ᒫᓕᒧᑦ, ᖁᔭᓐᓇᒦᒃ ᐅᑉᐱᕇᓐᓇᓚᐅᕋᕕᖕᒐ ᑎᑎᕋᖅᐸᑦᓕᐊᑎᑦᑐᖕᒐ.
ᐊᓈᓇᓐᓄᑦ, ᐊᑖᑕᓐᓄᑦᓗ, ᐊᒻᒪᓗ ᓯᐊᑉᒧᑦ ᓇᒡᓕᒃᑎᒃᑲ.
ᐊᓈᓇᑦᓯᐊᓐᓄᑦ, ᐊᑖᑕᑦᓯᐊᓐᓄᑦ, ᐊᑲᓐᓄᑦᓗ ᐋᓕᓐᒧᑦ. ᑦᓵᑦᒧᑦ.
ᑕᐃᒃᑯᓄᖕᒐᓕᒫᖅ ᐊᖅᑯᓵᖅᐸᒃᑐᓄᑦ.
ᑐᕉᒡᔅ-ᑲᓄᑦ ᑲᐃᐅᓪ, ᓂᑮᑕ, ᐋᑕᒻ, ᓕᕙᐃ, ᐊᒻᒪᓗ ᐄᐊᓐ. ᓇᒡᓕᒋᕙᑦᓯ.
Hᐃᐊᓄᕆᒧᑦ, ᑐᕋᐃᒧᑦ, ᐊᒻᒪᓗ ᐱᓕᐱᒧᑦ. ᐃᓚᓕᒫᓐᓄᑦ.
ᑕᐃᒃᑯᓄᖕᒐ ᐊᒃᓱᕈᖅᓯᒪᔪᓄᑦ ᒫᓐᓇᓗ ᐊᒃᓱᕈᖅᑐᓄᑦ.
ᑕᒪᓐᓇ ᐊᓂᒍᕐᓂᐊᕐᒥᔭᕗᑦ.
ᐊᑦᓗᖅᑕᕐᓗᑕ ᓯᕗᒧᑦ.

ᓇᒡᔨᒋᕙᑦᓯ,
ᔭᐃᒥᓯ

For Molly, thank you for believing in me every step of the way.
For my Mom and Dad and Zeb for loving me.
For Grandma, Grandpa, Danny, and Uncle Alan. For Chad.
For all those passed between now and then.
For my droogs Kyle, Nikita, Adam, Levi, and Ian. Nagligivagitsi.
For Henry, Dre, and Philippe. To all my relations.
To all of those who have suffered and suffer still.
We'll get through this.
One foot in front of the Other.

All my love,
Jamesie

Published by Inhabit Media Inc.
www.inhabitmedia.com
Inhabit Media Inc. (Iqaluit) P.O. Box 11125, Iqaluit, Nunavut, X0A 1H0 • (Toronto) 612 Mount Pleasant Rd., Toronto, Ontario, M4S 2M8

Design and layout copyright © 2023 Inhabit Media Inc.
Text copyright © 2023 Jamesie Fournier

Editors: Louise Flaherty, Neil Christopher, and Kelly Ward-Wills
Translator: Jaypeetee Arnakak
Art Director: Danny Christopher

ISBN: 978-1-77227-484-4

All rights reserved. The use of any part of this publication reproduced, transmitted in any form or by any means, electronic, mechanical, photocopying, recording, or otherwise, or stored in a retrievable system, without written consent of the publisher, is an infringement of copyright law.

Images:
cover: ronaldonene /Shutterstock.com, Danny Christopher, inside cover: SosnaRadosna/ Shutterstock.com, iii: Subhra De Mitra /Shutterstock.com, table of contents: gianni triggiani/ Shutterstock.com, page 10/11: ORebrik/Shutterstock.com, page 22/23: Yuri Kravchenk/Shuttersto com, page 40/41: piyaphong/Shutterstock.com, page 60-61: Shyjo/Shutterstock.com, page 80/81: Rich Carey/Shutterstock.com, page:98/99: Papin Lab/Shutterstock.com, 110/111: Pigdevil Photo/ Shutterstock.com, page 126: © 2023 Erica Jacque

This project was made possible in part by the Government of Canada.
Ce projet a été rendu possible en partie grâce au gouvernement du Canada.

We acknowledge the support of the Canada Council for the Arts for our publishing program.

Printed in Canada

Canada

Canada Council for the Arts
Conseil des Arts du Canada

ᔦᐃᒥᓯ ᕗᐊᓂᐊᐃ
Jamesie Fournier

ᑲᑎᖅᓱᒐᑦ
ELEMENTS

ᒧᒥᒃᑎᓇᔨ
ᔦᐃᐱᑎ ᐊᕐᓇᑲᒃ
Inuktitut translation by
Jaypeetee Arnakak

INHABIT
MEDIA

ᐃᓗᓕᖏᑦ

Table of Contents

ᐃᖅᑯᒻᒪᖅᐳᖅ—ᐊᐃᕙᔪᖅ

ᐃᖅᑯᒻᒪᖅᐳᖅ. ᓇᑎᖅ ᓂᓪᓕᓇᖅᐳᖅ. ᐃᒃᑮᓵᓗᖕᒑᒃ. ᐅᐃᒃᑲᒥ ᐃᓕᓴᖅᓇᖅᑐᒥᒃ ᖅᑭᓂᖅᐳᖅ. ᐃᓕᓴᖅᓇᖅᑐᖅᑲᖕᒋᓚᖅ. ᐅᐃᒻᒪᕈᔪᓕᖅᐳᖅ ᓂᐊᖅᑯᖕᒍᓪᓗᓂᓗ. ᖅᑲᐅᒪᑯᑖᑦ ᓯᕚᖅᐳᑦ. ᐃᒃᑮ. ᖅᑭᓂᖅᐳᖅ ᐊᑭᓯᖅᒥᒃ, ᖅᑭᐱᖕᒥᒃ, ᑭᓯᑐᐃᓐᓇᖅᒥᒃ ᐅᓕᒃᓴᒥᒃ. ᓇᓂᓯᖕᒋᓚᖅ. ᐊᒡᒐᖕᒐ ᐊᐅᒃᑲᖅᒥ ᖅᑭᓪᓕᖅᐳᖅ ᓇᑎᖅᒥ ᖅᑭᑯᖅᒥᒃ ᐊᒥᐊᖅᓯᒪᔪᖅ ᓯᐊᖅᓇᔮᖅᒥᒃ ᐊᒥᐊᖕᒐ ᖅᑲᐅᓕᖅᑐᖅ ᓯᓂᖕᒋᒍᑦ. ᓯᖅᑯᑦᑎᓕᖅᑐᖅ. ᖅᑯᖕᒐᓯᐊ ᑕᓯᒋᐊᖅᐹ ᓱᑲᑲᓪᓚᒃᐳᕐᓗ ᐋᖕᓂᖅᑐᓂ. ᑭᓯᖅᑲᖕᒋᑦᑐᖅ ᐃᓪᓗᕈᓯᖅ.

“ᓱᕙ...” ᖅᑲᐅᔨᒪᖕᒋᓚᖅ ᓇᒦᓪᒪᖕᒑᖅᒥ, ᑭᓯᐊᓂᓕ ᑲᖕᒌᓱᒃᐳᖅ ᓇᒦᒋᐊᖕᒐ. ᑲᑉᐱᐊᑦᑕᓕᖅᐳᖅ ᖅᑲᐅᔨᕙᓪᓕᐊᓕᖅᒥ. ᖅᑲᐅᔨᒪᐅᔭᐃᓐᓇᖅᐳᖅ ᑕᕝᕗᖕᒐᓛᖅᓂᖅᒥᓂᒃ. ᐃᓕᕋᑦᑕᒃᐳᖅ ᐃᒻᒥᓂᒡᓗ ᑕᓗᕈᒃᑯᑎᓪᓗᓂ ᑭᓯᐊᓂᓕ ᐅᐱᓐᓇᕋᓂ. ᑕᐃᒪᐃᓐᓂᐊᖅᑐᒋᖅᑲᑦᑕᖅᐳᖅ. ᑕᕝᕗᖕᒐᓛᖅᓂᖕᒐ ᓇᓗᓇᓚᐅᖕᒋᓚᖅ, ᑭᓯᐊᓂᓕ ᐅᐸᓗᐃᔭᐅᕗᖅ. ᓱᖕᒪᓪᓕ ᒫᓐᓇ? ᐱᓐᓇᔭᑦᑎᐊᓚᐅᓴᓗᐊᖅᐳᖅ. ᐱᖅᕈᐊᖅᑭᓐᓂᖕᒋᑦᑑᓕᓗᐊᖅᑲᐃ . . . ᐊᐃ?

ᐃᖅᑲᐃᓕᖅᐳᖅ ᓇᓪᓚᖕᒐᓪᓗᓂ ᓂᐊᖅᑯᐊᓄᑦ ᐊᒃᓴᑳᑲᑕᓚᐅᖅᑐᖅ. ᓄᓇᓯᐅᑎᓄᑦ ᓄᖅᑲᖅᑕᖅᕕᐅᑉ ᒪᓂᓴᖕᒐᓂ ᐊᒃᓴᑳᑲᑕᓚᐅᖅᑐᖅ. ᒪᑭᒍᓐᓇᐃᓪᓕᓚᐅᖅᑐᖅ. ᓄᔭᖕᒋᑦ ᓱᐅᖅᑭᓚᐅᖅᑐᑦ. ᓲᖅᓗ ᖅᑲᐃᖅᑲᒃᓴᐅᑎᒍᑦ ᓂᐊᖅᑯᐊᓄᑦ ᐊᒃᓴᓕᒃᑐᖅ. ᐊᖕᒋᖅᓴᖅᓴᓱᒃᑐᖅ ᐅᓇ. ᐅᖅᑲᓪᓚᒐᓱᒃᑲᓗᐊᖅᒥ ᐅᖅᑲᕈᓐᓇᖕᒋᓐᓇᒥ ᐅᖓᓗᑐᐃᓐᓇᖅᐳᖅ. ᓂᓪᓕᖅᓂᓕᒫᖅᒋᑦ ᖅᑲᐳᐊᖅᑯᔨᕙᑦ ᐊᖅᑭᐊᕈᐊᓂᑦ. ᓂᓪᓕᐊᕈᓘᔭᖅᐳᖅ ᓲᐳᖅᑐᓂ ᐃᓪᓚᖅᑲᓚᒃᐳᕐᓗ ᓲᖅᓗ ᐲᔭᐃᓇᓱᒃᑐᖅ ᓄᕙᖕᒥᒃ. ᒪᑭᒋᐊᖅᔫᒥᒐᓗᐊᖅᒥ, ᐅᐃᔾᔨᖕᒍᓕᑐᐃᓐᓇᖅᐳᖅ. ᔫᖅᑯᖅᑐᓂ ᒪᑭᒐᓱᒃᑲᓗᐊᖅᐳᖅ, ᑭᓯᐊᓂᓕ ᐅᖅᕉᔭᒥ ᓯᓚ ᐊᔭᐅᒐᖅᑎᒍᑦ ᐃᓗᐊᓂᒃ ᐊᒃᓴᓗᐊᖅᑲᖕᒋᑦᑐᑐᑦ ᐅᕕᔭᑉᐳᖅ. ᐊᖕᒋᖅᓴᖅᓴᓱᒃᑲᓗᐊᖅᐳᖅ. ᑕᒪᓐᓇ ᑲᕙᖅᐹ ᓄᖅᑲᖅᑯᕚᓗ.

ᐋᖕᒐᑦᑐᕈᓗᒃ. ᐋᖕᒐᕕᒡᔪᐊ

Awake—Argument

Awake. The floor is cold. Damn cold. His eyes sought the familiar. Nothing. Confusion and headache set in. Fluorescent lights buzzed. Cold. He reached for a pillow, a blanket, anything. Nothing. His hand glistened across the concrete painted dull grey and chipping at the edges. Flaking. He craned his neck and it tightened with pain. Nothing.

"What the . . . " He didn't know where he was, but deep down he was afraid he knew. The dawning horror of his surroundings. Somewhere he always feared he'd end up. He was afraid and ashamed, but not surprised. He had expected as much from himself. It was just a matter of time, but not now. Why now? Things had been going so well. Nothing bad had happened . . . right?

He could remember his head lolling on the ground. Rotating and grinding against the gravel of the parking lot. Trying to get up. Dirt caking into his hair. Sandpaper against scalp. Trying to get home. Trying to talk but all that came out was spit. Each syllable bubbled out of the furnace of his belly. He rasped and hissed and giggled like an asthmatic snake. He tried lifting his head, but it spun out. He tried working his knees, but they buckled and betrayed him and sent him spiralling in loops like a busted shopping cart. Trying to get home. Trying to make it all stop.

Drunk. Dead drunk you bastard.

ᓄᓇᓯᐅᑎᐅᑉ ᖃᐅᒪᖏᑦ. ᓄᓇᓯᐅᑎ ᖃᐅᒻᒪᒃᑎᑦᑎᕗᖅ ᓄᖅᑲᖓᕕᖕᒥᒃ, ᑖᑉᓲᒧᖓᓗ ᑐᕋᖓᖕᒪᑕ, ᒪᑭᓪᒐᖅᑐᖅ ᑕᕐᕋᓕᐅᖅᐳᖅ. ᓴᖅᑭᑕᐅᕗᖅ. ᐊᓚᒃᑲᖅᐳᖅ. ᑕᕐᕋᑯᑖᖓ ᐅᕙᖓᖅᑰᔨᕗᖅ, ᑕᓯᓯᒪᔪᖅ. ᐊᒪᕈᕋᓛᖅ ᐃᓪᓚᕐᕖᓕᑦᑎᔪᖅ ᑐᓵᙳᐊᖅᐹ. ᓄᓇᓯᐅᑎᒥᑦ ᒪᖀᕖᓕᑦᑎᔫᒃ ᒪᑐᐃᖅᓯᔫᒃ ᒪᑐᓯᔫᓪᓗ. ᖃᐅᒪᓂᕐᒥ ᑕᕐᕋᖓ ᓯᒍᓂᐊᓃᑉᐳᖅ ᓄᓇᓯᐅᑎᐅᑉ, ᐅᔾᔨᕆᒐᒥᐅᓪᓗ ᑕᒪᑐᒥᖓ ᐊᑲᐅᓯᕚᓪᓕᖅᐳᖅ. ᐃᓪᓚᖅᓯᑳᓪᓚᒃᐳᖅ ᓄᖅᑲᖅᑕᕐᕕᐅᑉ ᒪᓕᕋᖓᓂᒃ ᓂᖅᑐᐃᖅᑰᔨᓕᕐᒪᑦ ᐃᓪᓚᖅᐳᕐᓗ ᓂᐱᑭᑦᑐᓂ.

"ᖃᓄᐃᑉᐱᓪᓕ ᐅᓐᓅᔭᖅ, ᐊᖑᑏ?" ᑖᓐᓇ ᐃᓚᖅᐳᖅ. ᐃᓪᓚᐅᔭᐃᓐᓇᖅᐳᖅ. ᓂᐱᖓ ᐅᖓᓯᒃᐳᖅ ᐋᓪᓚᐅᓪᓗᓂ, ᓇᓗᓕᐅᖅᑲᔭᖅ ᐅᖅᑲᓪᓚᒋᐊᒃᓴᖅ. ᐃᓪᓚᖅᐳᖅ ᑕᕝᕙ ᑐᑭᓯᖓᒥ. ᑐᑭᓯᐅᒪᑦᑎᐊᕐᒥ. ᑕᐃᒻᒪᐃᓐᓂᐊᓚᐅᕐᒪ ᖃᖓᑐᐃᓐᓇᖅ. ᐃᓪᓚᙱᑲᐃᓐᓇᓚᐅᕐᓕ. ᑕᒪᓐᓇ ᑲᒪᒋᔭᐅᖕᒪᑦ. ᐃᓗᐊᒍᑦ ᐃᑯᒻᒪᒃᓴᐃᕗᖅ, ᑭᖑᓪᓕᖅᐹᑦᑎᐊᕐᒥᒃ ᐊᓗᐊᕐᒥᒃ ᐃᒋᑦᑎᕗᖅ ᐅᖅᑲᐅᓯᓪᓗ ᐃᑯᐊᓚᔪᑦ ᐊᓂᑎᑉᐸᐃᑦ.

"ᐊᖏᕐᕋ . . . ᕋᓱᒃᑐᖓ . . . ᐱᓱᒍᓐᓇᐃᓪᓕᒐᒪ . . . "

ᓂᐱᖓ ᖃᑎᑐᖕᒪᑦ ᑲᒪᐃᖅᑭᒃᐳᖅ, ᑐᑭᓯᕗᕐᓗ ᖃᓄᐃᓕᕐᒪᖔᑦ. ᐅᓇ ᓯᓂᓕᐊᑕᕿᓕᖅᑐᖅ. ᐋᖓᔅᓴᓗᐊᓕᖅᑐᖅ. ᐃᒥᐊᓗᖕᒧᑦ ᓵᓚᐅᔭᖅ. ᐊᑯᓂᐅᔅᓵᔭᓐᓃᖅᐳᖅ. ᑕᕝᕙᓕ ᑕᐃᒪ. ᐃᓗᐊᒍᑦ ᐅᖅᑲᓪᓚᒃᐳᖅ ᐋᖓᑦᑐᖅ:

ᑕᕝᕙ ᐱᔭᓇᐊᖅᑲᓕᖅᐳᖓ ᓴᐱᓕᕐᓗᖕᓘᓐᓃᑦ. ᓈᒻᒪᒋᓕᕈᑦ, ᐃᕐᓃᒃ. ᐊᑕᖅᑭᒍᓱᖕᓂᖅᓴᐅᕗᖅ ᑕᐃᓖᒃ.

ᐃᕝᕙᕈᓗᒃ. ᓱᓕᓚᐅᖅᑐᖅ ᐃᓐᓇ, ᓱᓕᐅᔭᐃᓐᓇᖅᑐᖅ ᐃᓐᓇ. ᓄᖅᑲᓕᕆᑦ. ᓵᓚᐅᓃᑦ ᓈᒻᒪᒋᓕᕈ. ᓴᐱᓕᓕᕆᑦ.

ᒪᑭᒥᑦ. ᓇᖏᖅᓯᑎᑕᐅᕗᖅ ᖅᑭᙵᖅᐳᕐᓗ ᓄᓇᓯᐅᑎᐅᑉ ᖃᐅᒪᖏᓐᓂ. ᐱᔪᓐᓇᖅᓯᔾᔫᒥᒐᒥ ᐃᒻᒥᓂᒃ ᓇᖏᕈᓐᓇᖅᓯᕗᖅ, ᑭᓯᐊᓂ ᐊᑯᓂᐅᙱᑦᑐᖅ ᐱᔪᓐᓇᐃᓪᓕᓂᐊᕐᒥᔪᖅ. ᐃᑉᐱᒋᕚᒃ ᐊᓪᓚᐅᑎᖏᒃ ᑎᒍᔭᐅᓚᒥᒃ ᑐᓄᐊᓂ ᐊᑦᑐᖏᖅᑕᐅᔪᑦ. ᓱᑲᑖᓘᒃ. ᓱᑲᖓᓗᐊᖅᐹᒃ ᒪᒃᑯᒃᑑᑉ ᐅᕙᓂᐊᓄᑦ. ᐳᑭᖅᑕᓕᐊᓗᐃᑦ.

The headlights. The headlights beamed across the parking lot, outlining his mutated silhouette. Exposing him. Revealing him. His elongated shadow off centre, askew. The Jackal cackled behind his mind. Two car doors opened and shut. His shade sat amiably across the hood, somewhat delighted by the situation. That laugh escaped through the boy's teeth as he worshipped the tarmac gods in little giggles.

"How are we doing tonight, sir?" Laughing. He was always laughing. His own voice far and foreign, lost trying to conjure words. He laughed because he understood. Understood all too well. Bound to happen sooner or later. He had to stop laughing. That was throwing them off. Deep inside he stoked the fires, threw on the last bit of coal, and felt burning words dredge out of him.

"Home . . . I'm trying . . . can't . . . walk . . . "

The deepness of his voice startled him, and he knew what that meant. He was shutting down. Going into autopilot. The spirits got him. Wouldn't be long now. The jig is up. The voice drawled inside of him:

Time to put up or shut up. Accept it now, son. Be more respect in it that way.

Bastard. He was right, he always was. Yield. Accept defeat. Give up.

Up. He was hauled onto his feet and his eyes squinted in the glare of the headlights. He mustered enough strength to stand on his own, but he knew that wasn't going to last. He felt his wrists bend behind his back and clamp down. Tight. Too damn tight on soft flesh. Fucking cops.

ᓵᓚᐅᓃᖅ ᓈᒻᒪᒋᓕᕈᒃ, ᐃᕐᓃᒃ. ᑕᐃᒫᒃ ᐱᐅᓂᖅᓴᐅᓂᐊᖅᑐᖅ.

“ᓇᒥ ᐊᖏᕐᕋᖅᑲᕋᕕᑦ, ᐊᖑᑏ?” ᖃᐅᔨᒪᒍᓐᓃᓕᖅᐳᖅ. ᐱᓂᐊᓕᖅᑐᖅ ᐃᖅᑲᐅᒪᙱᓪᓗᓂ.

ᕿᓗᐊᕐᓗᓯ ᖃᖓᑕᓲᕐᒥ ᐃᑭᒪᔪᓯ, Hᐃ’Hᐃ’!

“Hᐋ Hᐃ’ . . . ”

“ᐊᖒᑦ?”

“. . . ᐃᕝᕕᕈᓗᒃ . . . ”

“ᐊᖑᑏ, ᐅᕐᖃᐅᑎᒍᓇᖅᐱᑎᒍᑦ ᐊᑎᕐᓂᒃ?”

ᖃᐅᒻᒪᒃᑕᔩᕐᒧᑦ ᕐᑯᑖᓂᑦ ᖃᐅᒻᒪᓯᕕᐅᕗᖅ, ᓲᕐᓗ ᐅᓇ ᐃᓄᙳᐊᖅ ᐱᑰᑕᕐᒧᑦ ᐊᑕᐅᓯᕐᒧᑦ ᓂᕕᖓᓕᖅᑐᖅ.

ᑕᕝᕙ ᐱᔭᓇᐊᖅᑲᓕᖅᐳᑎᑦ ᓴᐱᓕᕐᓗᑎᓪᓘᓐᓃᑦ, ᐃᕐᓃᒃ.

“ᐊᖑᑏ . . . ” ᑭᐅᙱᓚᖅ. ᓄᓇᓯᐅᑎᐅᑉ ᒪᑐᐊ ᒪᑐᑲᓪᓚᒃᑕᐅᕗᖅ. ᓯᕗᒧᑦ ᐃᑦᑐᐊᖅᓴᓕᖅᐳᖅ ᑎᒍᔭᐅᕕᖕᒥ. ᓄᓇᓯᐅᑎ ᐊᐅᓚᔾᔭᒃᐳᖅ.

ᑭᐳᓯ ᑐᖅᑯᖅᓯᒪᑦᑎᐊᕐᓗᑕᐅᒃ! ᐊHᐋHᐃ’!

“ᓇᒥ ᐊᖏᕐᕋᖅᑲᕐᒪᖔᖅᐱᑦ ᐅᕐᖃᐅᑎᒍᓐᓇᖅᐱᑎᒍᑦ, ᐊᖑᑏ?” ᑭᐅᙱᓚᖅ. “ᐃ’ᐄ. ᑎᒍᕈᓗᓕᕐᓚᕗᒃ. ᓯᓂᓕᐊᑕᕐᕿᕈᓗᖕᓂᐊᕐᒪᑦ ᑕᐃᒫᒃ ᐊᕐᑭᑦᑐᖓᓴᖓᔪᒃᑐᖅ.”

ᐱᔭᓇᐊᖅᑲᓕᖅᐳᑎᑦ ᓴᐱᓕᕐᓗᑎᓪᓘᓐᓃᑦ, ᓄᑲᑉᐱᐊᖅ.

ᓯᕗᒧᑦ ᓯᓚᒧᑦ ᐃᑦᑐᐊᖅᓴᖅᐳᖅ ᐅᓐᓅᑉ ᑖᕐᓂᖓᓄᑦ ᑕᓕᓕᖅᑐᖅ. ᑖᕐᓂᕐᒧᑦ ᐄᔭᐅᓕᖅᑐᖅ. ᐊᖏᕐᕋᕈᒪᑐᐃᓐᓇᕋᓗᐊᖅᑐᖓᓕᑕ, ᐃᓱᒪᕗᖅ. ᖃᓄᐊᓗᒃᓕ ᑕᐃᒪᐃᓕᕙ? ᐱᓇᔭᑦᑎᐊᖅᑲᐅᕚᓗᐊᕐᓕ. ᕐᑯᕕᐊᓱᑦᑎᐊᖅᑲᐅᔪᖅ ᐃᒥᖅᑐᓂ. ᖃᓄᕐᓕ ᐃᒪᐃᓕᖄᓪᓚᑉ?

Accept defeat, son. It'll be better that way.

"Where do you live, sir?" He was shutting down. Autopilot checking in.

Make sure all seat belts are tightly fastened, Hehe!

"Haheh . . . "

"Sir?"

". . . bastard . . . "

"Sir, can you tell us your name?"

Flashlights lit his downturned face, a marionette on his last string.

Time to put up or shut up, son.

"Sir . . . " Nothing. The door slammed shut on the cruiser. He looked up from behind chicken wire. The car shifted into gear.

All tables in their upright and locked positions! Ahaheh!

"Can you tell us where you live, sir?" Nothing. "Fuck it. Let's take him in. He can sleep it off if he wants to dummy up."

Put up or shut up, boyo.

He stared blankly through the windshield into the oncoming night engulfing him. Swallowing him. *I just wanted to go home*, he thought. How'd this happen? Everything was going so well. He was having such a great time. How'd it come to this?

ᐊᖏᕐᕋᓕᖅᑐᒧᓪᓕ, ᓄᑲᑉᐱᐊᖅ. ᑕᐃᑲᓂᑐᐊᖅ ᐅᑕᖅᑭᓯᐅᕗᑎᑦ. ᐅᑕᖅᑭᓯᐅᕗᒍᒃ. ᑕᒪᓐᓇ ᖃᐅᔨᒪᔪᐃᑦ. ᑕᒪᓐᓇ ᖃᐅᔨᒪᔪᖓ. ᑕᐃᒪᐃᓐᓂᐊᓚᐅᕐᒪᑦ. ᐃᓂᑦᓚᒃᓴᐃᕗᒍᒃ, ᐃᓐᓇᖅᕕᓕᖅᓚᕗᒃ. ᐃᓇᖅᑲᐃ ᖃᖕᒍᑕᓲᕐᒥ ᐱᔨᑦᓯᖅᑎ ᐊᑭᓯᕐᒥᒃ ᖃᐃᑦᑎᔪᓐᓇᖅᐳᖅ! ᕼᐊᕼᐋ!

“ᕼᐋᕼᐃ’ . . . ”

ᐃᓐᓇᕈᓗᒃ. ᓱᓕᔪᕕᓂᖅ. ᓱᓕᐅᔭᐃᓐᓇᖅᑐᖅ.

We are going home, boyo. The one place that has been waitin' for ya. For us. You know it. I know it. It was just a matter of time. We made our bed, let us lie in it. Maybe the stewardess will have a pillow for our head! Haha!

"Haheh . . . "

Bastard. He was right. Always was.

Blood

I

ᖃᐃᕋᒃᑐᑦ ᐃᓄᒐᖖᒍᐊᑦ
ᐃᒪᕐᒥ ᐅᓂᐊᖅᑕᐅᕙᖅ.
ᕿᓪᓚᓇᒃᐸᑦ ᑕᕐᕋᑦ
ᐅᒥᐊᑉ ᐊᒥᖕᒐᓂ.
ᕿᖅᑯᐊᑦ ᐅᕐᕈᔮᕗᑦ ᐃᒪᕐᒥ.
ᐳᒃᑕᓛᖅᑐᑦ ᕿᔭᑦ ᐃᓇᑦᑎᕗᑦ,
        ᖃᓪᓕᕆᐊᓇᕐᓯ.
                ᖃᐃᓗᓯ ᖃᓪᓕᕆᐊᓇᕐᓯ.

ᓯᓂᖕᒥᑦ ᑎᒃᑕᐅᕋᓛᖅᐸᑦ.
ᒥᓗᒋᐊᖅ ᐃᓯᔾᔭᒃᐸᖅ ᑕᕐᕋᒥ.
ᐊᓪᒍᖅᓯᒪᔭᖅ. ᐃᒃᓴᓇᖅᑐᖅ.
        ᑕᐃᓐᓇ ᐱᔭᒥᓇᖅᑐᐊᓗᒃ.

ᑭᓪᓕᖅᑕᒃᑭᑦ ᑮᓇᐃᑦ ᐆᒪᓂᖕᒋᑦ, ᓇᕈᔮ.
ᓴᓪᓗᓂᖅ ᐳᑐᓚ.
ᓴᔭᒃᑕᖅᑐᖅ ᐅᓂᒃᑳᖅ ᓇᕿᑦᑎᕕᓪᓚᐊᕗᑦ ᑭᓗᒃᑯᑦ.

ᓂᓪᓚᖖᒋᓪᓗᑎᑦ.
ᐃᓄᒐᖖᒍᐊᖅᐱᑦ ᐊᑯᓐᓂᖕᒋᒍᑦ ᐅᓇᓗᒋᑦ.
ᐃᐱᒃᓴᐅᑎᒋᒃᑭᑦ ᑐᕐᑯᖕᒐᔭᑦ ᓴᐅᓂᕕᓂᖕᒋᑦ.
ᑭᒍᑎᑎᑦ ᓈᓴᒃᑭᑦ.
        ᑐᒃᓯᐊᓇᑦ ᓯᓚᓗᑕᕐᑯᓪᓗᒍ.

ᓂᐱᕋᓛᑦ ᓴᑲᕗᑦ ᐃᔾᔭᕐᒧᑦ.
ᑐᒃᑲᖅᐸᑦ ᓯᐅᕋᕐᒥᒃ ᑕᕐᕋᐅᑉ ᖁᓛᒍᑦ.
ᐃᓱᒪᓂᕐᓗᐃᕗᑦ ᒪᓂᕋᕐᒥᒃ ᓇᖕᒋᕐᕕᒋᓚᐅᖅᑕᕐᓂᒃ.
ᓴᑲᕗᑦ,
        ᕙᐃ!
                ᕙᐃ!
                        ᕙᐃ!
ᐅᒥᐅᑉ ᐃᓗᐊᓂ.

I

Smooth fingers
lurk beneath the waves.
Astral patterns
flutter across the hull.
The drunken kelp sways.
The deadheads beckon,
Closer.
Come closer.

The peripheries titter.
Leech murmurs from the shadows.
Disjointed.   Seductive.
That heady allure.

Cut the quick of faces, pilgrim.
Tunnel deceit.
The twitching lore burrowing between the seams.

Bite your tongue.
Spit between your fingers.
Whet the bones of dead men.
Count your teeth.
Pray for rain.

Little voices chant onto the loam.
Kicking dirt over shadow.
Cursing the ground where once you stood.
Chanting,
Fie!
Fie!
Fie!
Underneath the hood.

II

ᐊᓄᖀᖅᐳᖅ. ᓯᐅᕋᖅ ᓇᑎᕈᕕᐊᖅᐳᖅ,
ᓴᖅᑭᑎᑦᑎᓪᓗᓂ ᐱᕈᖅᑐᕕᓂᑐᖃᕐᓂᒃ
ᑐᖁᓕᓯᒪᔪᓂᒃ.

ᕿᑭᖅᑰᓚᑦ ᑕᖅᑲᒧᑦ.
ᐃᓕᓗᒍ ᕿᑐᑦᑐᒐᐅᔭᖅ ᓇᑎᕐᒧᑦ.
ᓯᓂᓕᐅᕐᓕ ᕿᐱᒃ
ᐃᒧᓗᒍᓗ.

ᐋᓯᕙᑦ ᓯᓂᖅᑲᑎᒥᒃᑭᑦ, ᐃᕐᓃᒃ.
ᐹᕐᖑᓚᑦ ᓄᓇᕋᑦ ᐊᑖᒍᑦ.
ᓂᐊᖁᐃᑦ ᐊᒃᓴᓕᒍᑦ ᐃᔾᔪᕐᒥ.
ᒪᕐᓚᑦᑐᑦ ᐄᓪᒪᑎᑦ ᑭᐅᔪᓐᓇᙱᑦᑕᑦ.

ᐅᓇ ᒥᖑᐊᖅᓯᒪᔪᖅ ᐊᓕᒍᖅ ᒪᓕᒃᐳᖅ ᓴᐸᖓᓂᒃ ᐅᔭᒥᒥᒃ.
ᐊᓗᒃᑐᖅᐳᖅ ᐅᖅᓱᓂᒃ ᑕᖅᑲᓂᒃ.
ᐃᒃᓱᒍᖕᓂᖅ ᑕᕝᕙᐅᒐᖅ.

ᓱᖅᑕᐅᒐᖅ ᐃᖅᑲᐅᒪᓈᙱᑦᑐᒧᑦ.
ᐅᓪᓗᒧᑦ ᐱᓂᕐᓗᒃᑕᐅᓯᒪᔭᐃᓐᓇᐅᒐᒍᑦ, ᐊᐃ?
ᐱᐅᔪᖅ, ᑎᑕᒃ, ᑕᑯᒥᓇᓕᐊ,
ᕿᒃᓵᒃᐳᑦ ᑲᐅᒃᑕᐅᑦ ᑲᓱᖕᒪᑦ.

II

Wind blows. Grains trundle,
uncovering skeletal gardens
gone to seed.

Slink into the shadows.
Lay the cardboard down.
Pleat the sleeping bag
and fold.

Sleep with the spiders, son.
Crawl underneath the flowers.
Grind your head into the dirt.
                    Mired hearts won't reply.

This tallowed glass clocks a beaded chain.
Licks greasy shadows.
Lascivious remains.

Destroyed beyond memory.
Daylight victims, aren't we all?
Beauty, music, art,
                    mourns the hammer's fall.

III

ᓯᒡᒐᓕᐊᑦ ᐊᓇᕐᕕᖕᒥ.
ᐅᓗᒃᓴᐅᑦ ᐃᒐᓛᑉ ᐃᓕᔾᔨᕕᖕᒐᓃᑉᐳᖅ.
ᐳᐃᒍᖅᑕᐃᓕᒋᑦ
ᐱᓇᓱᐊᕈᓐᓇᕐᓂᖅ ᓵᓚᒋᓗᒍ.

ᑕᕐᕋᖅᑕᕐᑲᖅᐳᖅ ᐃᒡ ᓘᑉ ᕐᑭᓚᖕᒐᓂ.
ᓲᐴᖅᑑᑉ ᐃᔅᓯᖕᒐ ᐊᑭᓐᓇᕐᒦᑉᐳᖅ.
ᓯᓚᓪᓕᕗᑦ ᓯᓂᒃᑐᐃᓐᓇᐅᕗᑦ
ᐃᖅᑲᖅᓴᖅᑎᓪᓗᖕᒐ
ᐱᔭᕆᐊᕐᑲᓚᐅᖅᑕᓐᓂᒃ.
ᐃᓱᒪᒋᔭᕆᐊᑐᓚᐅᙱᑦᑐᓂᒃ.
ᒫᓐᓇᓕ ᐱᑕᕐᑲᕈᓐᓃᖅᑐᖅ,
ᕐᑲᐅᔨᕗᖕᒐ,
ᐅᓇ ᑎᒥ
ᐱᕙᓐᓇᙱᑦᑐᖅ.

ᑰᓐᓇᒃᓯᒪᕙᖅ ᐹᕐᓕ.
ᐃᐱᒃᓴᕈᒃ ᓄᑖᕐᒥᒃ.
ᕐᑲᐳᐊᒃᓯᒪᕙᖅ ᐃᕐᑭᖕᒥᒃᑎᒍᑦ..
ᐊᑏ, ᐃᑉᐱᒍᓱᕐᑲᑎᕐᑲᕆᑦ.
ᓯᕗᒧᓕᕆᑦ,
ᓇᐃᑉᐱᑦᔪᒋᑦ ᕐᑭᓚᕈᑎᒥᒃ ᐃᒧᓯᒪᕙᒥᒃ.
ᒥᖅᓱᒃᑭᑦ ᐅᓪᓗᕆᐊᑦ.

ᐅᓇ ᓱᓇᒃᑯᑖᖅ ᓵᓚᒋᓇᓱᒃᑕᐃᓕᐅᒃ.
ᑕᑎᒋᒍᒃ, ᑖᓐᓇ ᐱᔭᐃᑦ.
ᓵᑖᓇᓯ ᐃᔨᖅᓯᒪᕗᖅ ᑎᑎᖅᑲᑦ ᐃᓗᓕᖕᒋᓐᓂ.
ᕐᑯᔭᓈᖅᑕᐅᓯᒪᕙᖅ,
ᐅᓪᓗᕆᐊᖅᑲᙱᑦᑐᖅ ᐊᑯᓐᓂᕗᑦ.

III

Cigarettes in the bathroom.
Pomace on the sill.
Do not forget
to defeat the will.

There's a shadow on the ceiling.
Nicotine in the walls.
The neighbours are all sleeping
as I try to recall
something I had to do.
Something I had to ignore.
Now that there is nothing,
I realize,
this corps
does not hold.

Take off the edge.
Hone a new blade.
Foaming at the corners.
Please, commiserate.
Move on,
find a new ball of string.
Quilt stars.

Do not attempt to defeat this feature.
Trust, you received this.
The devil's in the details.
Abandoned,
starless amidst.

IV

ᑲᐅᒃᑐᑭᑦ ᐅᑯᐊ ᑭᑭᐊᑦ
ᐅᖃᓚᒫᖅᑕᐅᔪᑦ ᑐᖁᖓᔪᓂᑦ.
ᐊᒻᒪ ᑎᒍᒻᒥᔪᖅ, ᓄᕿᑦᑕᔪᒃᑐᖅ,
ᐃᓗᖕᒧᑦ ᑑᖅᑐᖅ.
ᐃᓱᒫᓗᙱᑦᑐᖅ ᓴᖅᑮᔭᖅᑐᓂᓗ.
ᐃᑉᐱᖕᓂᐊᙱᓚᖅ ᑖᒃᑯᓂᖓ ᐃᑭᖕᒥᓐᓂᒃ?
ᑲᐅᒃᑐᕈ ᐅᔭᕋᑦᑎᐊᖅ.

ᑲᐅᒃᑐᖅ
        ᑲᐅᒃᑐᖅ
                ᑲᐅᒃᑐᖅ

ᐃᓯᕙᒃᑭᑦ ᐊᒻᒪᑎᑦ, ᑯᑐᒃᑐᑦ
ᐊᐅᐸᖅᑐᒥᒃ ᐱᐅᔪᒥᑦ.

ᖁᖕᒪᕆᑦ
        ᖁᖕᒪᕆᑦ
                ᖁᖕᒪᕆᑦ

ᐅᓚᐅᑉ ᐃᓗᐊᓂ.

ᐅᐃᒃ, ᓯᖕᒪᑦ ᐃᑭᖃᖅᐸᑦ?
ᓯᕿᙳᔭᖅ ᓯᕗᓂᖅᐸᒃᑑᒐᓗᐊᖅ ᑭᓯᐊᓂᓚ ᑲᓯᒃᑐᙱᓚᖅ.
ᕿᕙᐊᖅᓂᑕᓛᑦ—ᓅᑉᐸᒃᑐᖅ.
ᑕᕝᕙᓚ, ᐃᑲᖃᖅ ᐊᓯᕈᙱᓚᖅ.
ᐅᐃᕐᖕᒐᒃᓴᐅᑦ ᖃᐅᒪᓂᖅ ᖄᔪᖕᓇᖅᐳᖅ.
ᓯᕈᐃᕗᖅ ᓴᕙᖅᓴᖕᒥᒃ,
ᐃᒧᓪᓗᐃᕗᖅ ᓇᓂᕐᐅᑉ ᑕᓗᖓᓂᒃ.
ᓱᐴᖅᑑᑉ ᐃᔅᓯᖓ ᖃᒃᑭᓐᓇᖅᐳᖅ

IV

Tack down these nails
read from the dead.
Clenched in a fist, tetanic,
thrust inward.
Indifferent and on display.
Impervious to these wounds?
Bring the hammer down.

Boom
        Boom
                Boom

Unfurl your fingers, dripping
the red from the good.

Smile
        Smile
                Smile

Underneath the hood.

        Husband, what wounds are these?
        The clock strikes but never ticks.
        Every time I look—it moves.
        Yet, the hour remains the same.
        The opiate light dissuades.
        Tarnishes the brass,
        crimps the lampshade.
        Nicotine stains taste bitter

ᓲᕐᓇᖅᐳᖅ
ᓲᕐᓇᖅᐳᖅ
ᓲᕐᓇᖅᐳᖅ

ᐋᓐᓂᕐᓇᖅᐳᖅ ᓱᓕᐃᔭᖅᑕᐅᓪᓗᓂ.
ᐳᓚᒥᓚᐅᖅᐳᖓ. ᐱᐅᙱᑦᑐᖅ.
ᐅᐸᒃᐳᖓ ᓇᐸᔪᕐᒧᑦ ᓱᕿᒃᓯᒪᔪᕐᒧᑦ
ᑕᕐᕿᑦ ᒧᒥᖅᑐᑦ ᐊᐅᓚᕗᑦ
ᐅᒥᐅᑉ ᐃᓗᐊᓂ.

Sweet
        Sweet
                Sweet

It's painful to be de-feathered.
Blacked out. No good.
Driven to my broken tower
while twisted shadows writhe
        underneath the hood.

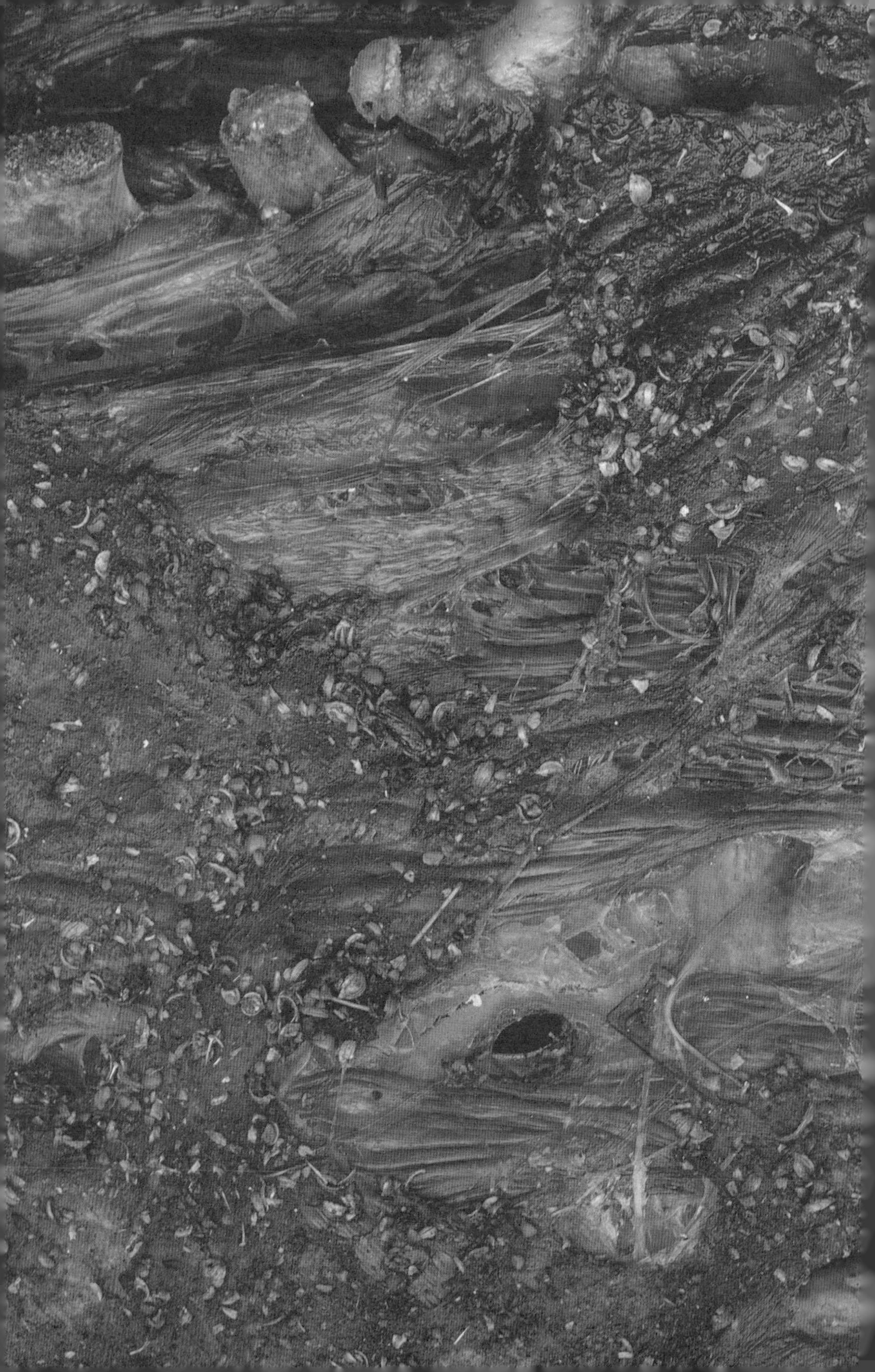

ᐃᕙᓗ
Sinew

ᐃᓐᓇᑐᖃᖅ

ᑐᖕᒍᔪᖅᑐᑦ ᓵᑦᑐᔮᑦ ᕿᓪᓕᖅᐳᑦ
ᕿᓪᓕᕐᓂᕐᒧᑦ ᐃᑭᓕᐅᖅᐳᑦ.
ᖄᕐᒧᑦ ᓴᓇᐅᒐᑦ ᐅᕕᓂᖕᒧᑦ ᐃᑭᓕᐅᖅᐳᑦ.
ᐅᖁ ᖁᖕᒐᑉᐳᖅ ᖁᓚᕐᓇᖅᓯᔪᒧᑦ.

ᐊᓈᓇᒪ ᐅᖃᐅᓯᖓ ᑐᓴᕐᓂᕆᕙᕋ,
ᓂᕆᓕᖅᑕᕐᒧᑦ ᓂᓪᓚᐅᑎᖕᒋᑦ ᐃᑎᓗᐊᕆᕙᒃᑲ.
ᓯᖁᑦᑎᕐᓃᑦ ᐳᑐᓯᕗᑦ ᑕᓗᒥᒃ
ᐋᖅᑭᒃᓯᓪᓗᑎᒃ ᐅᓪᓗᕆᐊᓂᒃ ᐱᖅᑯᓯᑐᖃᖕᒋᓐᓄᑦ.

    ᖃᑯᖅᑕᖅ ᑕᓕᖅᐱᖕᒥ.
    ᐃᓚᖕᒋᑦ ᐱᕗᑦ ᕿᓐᓂᖅᑕᒥᒃ.
    ᐃᒃᓯᕋᕐᔪᐊᑦ ᐃᔾᒋᕗᑦ ᓱᕈᓰᑦ ᐃᓂᖕᒐᓄᑦ.
    ᖃᕐᑭᐊᓕᕆᑦ ᐊᖕᒐᒃᑯᕐᒧᑦ ᐱᔪᓂᒃ.

ᐅᓕᒪᐅᒻᒧᑦ ᓴᓇᔭᐅᔪᖅ, ᑎᕝᔭᑦ ᑭᑉᐹᕆᒃᑐᑦ ᐊᔾᔭᖅᓯᕗᑦ
ᐊᒃᑕᖅᑕᐅᔪᒥᒃ ᐊᑕᓂᐅᓂᖅᒥᒃ.
ᐊᓐᓇᐅᒪᒋᑦ 10,000-ᖏᖅᓱᖅᑐᒥᒃ ᖁᓕᕇᖕᓂᓕᖕᒥᒃ
ᓂᓪᓛᓗᖕᒥᒃ ᐃᓄᖅᑭᓪᓗᑎᑦ.

ᑲᔾᔮᕆᕙᕋ ᓯᓚᖅᔪᐊᖅ ᐅᖓᑎᑦᑎᓐᓃᑦᑐᖅ,
ᑕᕐᓃᑦ ᐱᙳᐊᕐᕕᖕᒐᑦ.
ᐃᓄᖃᑖᕐᓄᑦ ᒪᑭᒪᑎᑕᐅᕗᖅ.
ᐅᓇ ᓱᒡᒑᔪᖅ ᓯᓚᐃᕐᕆᓯᓂᖅ.
ᐅᓇ ᐃᑯᐊᓚᔪᐊᓗᒃ ᓄᓇ
ᓱᓕ ᐃᑯᐊᓚᕗᖅ ᐅᓪᓗᒥᒧᑦ.
ᑭᓯᐊᓂᓕ ᑕᐃᒪ ᑕᕐᕋᑦ ᖃᐃᑉᐸᑕ ᓱᐱᓯᔪᖅᑐᕐᓗᑎᒃ ᐃᒐᒥᒃ
    ᐅᕙᑦᑎᓐᓂᒡᓗ ᓇᒃᓴᕐᓗᑎᒃ.

Long in the Tooth

Turquoise dominoes glisten
opal fire wounds.
Reliefs stone open flesh.
Rot smiling doom.

I love to hear my mother's tongue,
glottal beyond my depth.
Fragments pierce through the veil
to align the stars again.

White on the right.
Others take the black.
Bishops gaze kiddie-corner.
Shrive mystic acts.

Roughly hewn, driftwood dice bear
the slough cast for sovereignty.
Survive ten-thousand-fold
in frigid civility.

I love the world beyond,
where the spirits play.
The little people holding it all together.
This vicious masquerade.
This fiery landscape
endures unto this day.
'Til shadows come to dispel the hearth
and spirit us away.

ᑭᑦᑐᕋᖅᓯᒪᔪᑦ ᐃᕙᓗᑦ

ᑎᓕᒐᓂᐊᓚᒫᑦ ᐸᕝᕕᓴᒍᒪᕗᑦ ᐊᕿᒡᒋᕐᔪᐊᖃᕐᕕᖕᓂᒃ
ᓄᕗᔾᔨᕐᓂᕐᒧᑦ ᐃᓱᖅᓯᑎᓪᓗᒍ.
ᐃᒃᓚᒍᖕᓂᖅ ᓴᖅᑭᐸᐳᖅ ᖃᑯᖅᑖᒃ ᐃᔫᒃ
ᖁᒻᒧᑦ ᕿᕙᐊᖅᐴᒃ
ᖁᑖᓄᑦ
ᕿᓐᓂᕐᓂᐅᑉ.

ᐆᒻᒪᑎᓐᓄᑦ ᓯᖁᒥᓐᓇᖅᐳᖅ ᐃᒫᒃ ᐅᖃᓇᐊᒃᓴᖅ
ᑭᓯᐊᓂ ᑕᕝᕙ, ᓇᖕᒥᓂᓕᒐᕕᐅᒃ.
ᑕᒻᒪᓕᑦ ᓴᓇᙳᐊᒐᒃᓵᖅ, ᑎᒍᒥᐊᓕ ᐊᒃᓱᑦ ᓈᓴᐅᓯᓕᔾᔪᑎᓂᒃ
ᒪᓚᒃᑐᓂᒃ ᖃᐃᑦᓚᒫᕐᓂᐅᑉ ᕿᑭᖄᕐᓂᖕᒐᓂᒃ ᐊᓚᒃᑐᒥᒃ.
ᓴᙱᑦᓚᓴᖅᓯᒪᔪᖅ ᐃᒥᐊᓗᒃ ᓄᑐᕋᖅᐳᖅ.
ᐃᕋᒃᑏᑦ ᐅᖅᑲᒃᑲᓐᓂᖅᐳᑦ
ᓄᓇᕐᔪᐊᒥ ᑲᓪᓚᕐᓂᕐᒥᒃ.

ᐃᒥᖃᑎᒋᓚᐅᕐᒥᒃᑭᑦ ᓯᓚᐅᑉ ᐃᓄᖕᒋᑦ.
ᐆᔾᒥᐊᓇ ᓯᐃᑦ ᐱᖃᑎᒋᕙᕗᑦ.
ᐊᔪᓚᖅᓯᒪᓂᐅᑉ ᐃᑯᒪᖕᒐ ᐊᓗᒃᓯᕗᖅ
ᑐᖁᑦᑎᓪᓗᓂᓗ ᑕᐃᐊᓂᓴᔅᒥᒃ.

ᐃᒪᕋᓚᕝᕕᐅᑉ ᑭᓗᐊᓂ
ᓴᙱᔪᖅ ᐃᒻᒥᓂᒃ ᐊᑲᖅᓴᙱᓐᓂᖅ
ᐃᔾᔭᙳᑎᑦᑎᕗᖅ ᓯᓈᓂᒃ ᑕᑯᓐᓇᙳᐊᖅᓂᐅᑉ.
ᐊᐅᓚᑦᑎᕗᖅ ᑎᖅᑎᑦᑐᒥᒃ, ᐅᐃᒻᒪᐅᖅᑲᔪᒥᒃ ᐊᖓᔪᖅᑳᖑᓂᖅᒥᒃ
ᐊᒻᒧᑦ ᑖᕐᓂᐊᓗᖕᒧᑦ ᑕᓕᐅᕐᒥ!

ᐅᖅᑯᖕᒋᑦ ᐃᓅᓂᑦᑕ
ᐊᐅᒃᑎᑦᑎᕗᑦ ᓂᓚᖕᒥᒃ ᐃᒥᖅᑕᑦᑎᓐᓂ.
ᕿᓄᓇᖅᐳᖅ ᐃᕿᖕᒐᔪᖅ ᑕᑯᓐᓇᖅᑕᖅ.
ᕿᒃᓵᒍᑎᖃᖅᐳᖅ ᐊᓯᖅᑯᒃᑲᓴᖅᑐᒥᒃ.
ᐃᖅᑲᐅᑉ ᒪᕐᕋᓇᐆ ᐃᖅᑯᒪᓂᐅᑉ,
ᐃᓐᕋᖅᑐᖅᓂᒃᑯᑦ ᐊᑭᕋᖅᑐᖅᓂᑦ ᓯᕗᒧᐸᑦᓚᐊᕗᑦ,
ᐅᓇᑕᐅᑎᕗᑦ ᓂᓕᐅᒋᔅᑎᓐᓂ
ᐊᑭᕋᑦᑎᓐᓄᑦ ᑐᓂᔅᐅᕗᑦ, ᐊᖕᒋᕈᑕᐅᓚᐅᖅᑐᑦ ᓱᕋᑕᐅᓪᓗᑎᒃ.

Broken Sinews

Every fox needs a henhouse
when the clouds begin to murk.
A seedy pleasure corps where white eyes
roll
    over
        black.

It breaks my heart to say this
but hey, it's your dime.
Err serpentine, hold fast to functions
the period's sine prowls asunder.
Diluted spirits beckon.
Howlers respeak
    earthly thunder.

    Carouse the gods again.
    Rosemary Sweet is with us.
    Street lips lick the flame
    and kill Dionysus.

In the backs of bars
raucous self-loathing
gutters the precipice of revelry.
Driving a seething, riotous fiefdom
Down a sunless sea!

The lees of our humanity
rot the ice of our drink.
Bemoans the sinuous vision.
Laments potential missed.
The dregs of the waking world,
    cruel machinations soldier on,
our stock we have in fantasy
sorely betrayed, reneged upon.

ᓇᓗᓕᐅᖅᑲᓂᕐᒧᑦ ᓇᓗᓇᐃᒃᑯᑕᑦ

ᐃᓯᕙᑕᖅ ᐃᓪᓕᖅ ᐊᐅᓚᐅᑎᖅᑲᕐᕙᖕᒥ.
ᐃᖏᓗᐃᑦ ᓴᓂᐅᑏᓪᓗ.
ᑳᒪᕐᓃᑦ ᑕᖅᓴᐅᕗᑦ ᓇᑎᕐᒥ.
ᖏᐃᓂ ᑯᕙᔭᐅᔪᕙᓂᖅ ᐅᕐᕿᔮᔪᒧᑦ ᐅᐃᔾᔮᖅᑐᒧᑦ.

ᐅᕙᓂᒃ ᐊᐅᖕᓂᐅᕗᖅ ᐅᔭᕋᑐᑦ ᓄᓇᐅᑉ ᐃᑭᐊᖕᒪᓂᑦ.
ᓂᐅᖅᓯᓂᐅᕗᖅ ᑲᔾᔮᕈᓱᒃᑕᐅᑎᕆᔪᒥᒃ.
ᖁᒧᒃᓯᐅᑎᖕᒪᑕ ᐊᕐᑯᑦᑑᓪᓗ ᐊᑯᓐᓂᖕᒪᓂ,
ᖃᓄᖅ ᑕᐃᒪᐃᓕᓐᓂᖅᐸ?

ᐆᓇᕐᓂᐅᕗᖅ ᐊᐅᖕᒥ ᑕᓗᕈᒃᑯᑎᓂᕐᒥᓪᓗ.
ᐊᑕᓃᑦ ᐃᓚᓕᐅᑎᓯᒪᔪᓂᒃ, ᐱᕙᒃᑐᑦ ᓄᓇᓯᐅᑎᑯᑖᑦ.
ᐃᓵᖅᑲᖖᒋᑦᑐᑦ, ᐃᓱᒪᐃᒍᑎᓯᒪᔪᑦ, ᑕᓕᓯᒪᔪᑦ, ᖃᕿᐊᓕᖅᑐᑦ.
ᑕᑎᑐᕗᑦ ᓯᓚᓗᖕᓂᕐᒥ!
ᓱᖏᑦ ᐱᓇᓱᖕᓂᐊᖅᑕᖕᒋᑦ, ᖃᓄᖅ ᐱᓂᐊᕐᓂᕋᓕᕈᖏ?
ᓱᓇᐅᖏ ᐊᑭᖕᒐ ᑐᓴᕈᒥᓇᖅᑑᑉ ᖃᓄᑎᒋᓗ ᐃᑭᖅᑐᑎᖏ ᐃᔾᔪᖅ
ᐅᓂᐊᖅᑕᐅᓂᖕᒐ?
ᓇᓪᓕᐊᑦ 7 ᐃᑯᐊᓚᑎᑕᐅᔪᑦ ᓈᓚᖕᓂᐊᖅᐸᑦ ᓯᓚᕐᔪᐊᑉ ᓄᖑᓐᓂᖕᒐᓄᑦ?
ᓱᓇᑦ ᐃᓗᐊᖅᓴᐅᑎᐅᖏᑦ ᐃᖏᓗᓄᑦ ᑭᑦᑐᕋᖅᓯᒪᔪᓄᑦ?
ᓇᓪᓕᐊᑦ ᑕᐃᓐᓇ ᓄᕐᕋᖅ ᐱᓲᐊᓪᒥᐅᑦ ᑲᑕᓚᐅᖅᑐᖅ ᓱᖏᓕᑭᐊᖅᓴᖅᐸ
ᐅᖅᑲᐅᔭᕐᓂᒃ ᑲᑕᒐᖅᑐᓂᒃ
ᐅᓪᓛᒃᑯᑦ ᓯᑎᐱᓚᒥ?

Hesitation Marks

A cot in the machine room.
Sinew and broomsticks.
Droplets stain on the floor.
Wine bottle ellipsis.

A skin of molten trauma.
A draught of instant bliss.
'Tween the horse and the rider,
        how did it come to this?

A fever of blood and shame.
Patchwork lords, desperate train.
Eyeless, demented, concealed, repentant.
Wilful of the rains!
What the actions, what the vow?
What dread gospel and what rough plough?
What seven fires herald the last?
What balms broken sinews past?
What fell lamb of Bethlehem scorns
the leaves from the trees
        like September morn?

ᓇᒡᓕᒋᔭᕐᒧᑦ ᑎᑎᖅᑲᖅ, ᓯᓚᖅᑲᑎᒧᑦ

ᐃᓕᑉᐸᓪᓕᐊᕗᑎᑦ ᑕᒻᒪᖅᑲᑦᑕᖅᑕᕐᓂᑦ.
ᑭᔅᔭᐃᕗᑎᑦ ᑭᔅᔭᐃᓪᓗᑎᑦ.
ᖃᓂᓪᓕᒋᐊᕈᒃ ᐊᖏᓛᑦ, ᐃᕐᓃᒃ.
ᖃᐃᒥᑦ, ᓯᓚᐃᕐᓇᔨᐊᓘᒃ.

ᐊᑯᓐᓂᐊᓂ ᐱᓂᕐᓗᒃᑕᐅᔫᑉ ᐱᓂᕐᓗᒃᑑᓪᓗ.
ᑐᓂᔭᐅᔫᑉ ᐊᖅᓵᖅᑕᐅᔫᓪᓗ.
ᑖᒃᑯᐊᒃ, ᑐᑭᓯᐅᒪᓂᐅᑉ ᒥᒃᓵᒋᐊᕐᓂᖓᓂ,
ᓯᐊᕐᒪᒃᑕᐅᕖᒃ ᐃᑯᒪᒧᑦ?

ᐃᓱᒪᖅᓱᕐᓂᕐᒧᑦ ᐱᔪᓐᓇᕐᓂᐅᕗᖅ.
ᓯᕐᓈᕐᓂᖅ ᐊᒃᖢᐃᑦᑐᓄᑦ.
ᑖᒃᑯᐊ ᐱᑦᑎᐊᕈᓐᓇᙱᑦᑐᑦ, ᐳᕙᖅᐳᑦ ᐃᖏᐅᓕᒃᑐᑐᑦ,
ᓂᐱᖅᑲᑦᑐᑎᒃ ᑭᖑᓪᓕᖅᐹᑦᑐᑦ ᓱᐴᒐᑐᕐ!

ᐳᖅᑐᔪᑦ ᐃᒡᓗᑦ ᓯᕐᑯᑦᑎᖅᑕᐅᓕᕐ!
ᐱᑐᒡᕕᑦ ᑐᕐᑯᑦᑎᔪᓐᓇᖅᓯᓕᕐ!
ᐃᑳᕈᒃ ᐅᑉᐱᕐᓂᖅᑲᙱᑦᑐᑦ ᓄᓈ.
ᐊᖑᒃᑯᕐᒧᑦ ᐃᓄᐃᓪᓚᖅ!

ᓄᓇ ᑎᓪᓕᒃᑕᐅᕗᖅ ᐊᑕᓂᕐᓄᑦ, ᐊᒡᒍᖅᑕᐅᕗᕐᓗ ᑕᐃᒃᑯᓇᙵᑦ ᐱᒃᑯᓪᓕᕐᓄ
ᖀᒥᒃᑐᑦ ᐱᐅᔪᓇᔪᑦ. ᑐᙵᕙᖅᑲᙱᑦᑐᑦ ᐅᑉᐱᕐᓃᑦ.
ᐊᐅᓚᑕᐅᕗᑦ ᐃᔨᕋᖅᑐᕐᓂᒃᑯᑦ ᐱᓇᓱᖕᓂᕐᒧᑦ
ᔭᖅᑭᑦᑎᓚᐅᖅᑐᒧᑦ ᐊᑕᓂᐅᓂᕐᒥᒃ.

Love Letter, Neighbour

Armed with your mistakes.
        Scissor by scissor.
        Move your flint in closer, son.
                Come, great pretender.

Between the victim and the victor.
        The lost and the gained.
Are they, of imagination compact,
        both smudged by the flame?

The authority of the decadent.
        The wrath of the well-to-do.
The ne'er-do-wells, in a rising swell,
sound the last bassoon!

        Tear the towers down!
        Weaponize the chains!
        Traverse the heathen moor.
        The wilderness arcane!

Land stolen by the crown, parcelled by those proud
of self-righteous malignity.   Of unfounded piety.
With a diseased sense of insidious intent
that forced sovereignty.

ᑲᑎᓐᓂᐅᑉ ᐃᓐᓄᒃᑕᐅᓂᖓ:

- ᑎᑭᖄᖅᑐᕈᓗᒃ,
- ᐳᐃᒍᕐᓂᖃᕕᑦ:
  ᐊᑕᖅᑭᕐᓈᒃ, ᕐᑯᐃᓇᖕᓇᖅ.
- ᓰᖑᓂᐊᓗᒃ ᐱᐅᙱᑦᑐᖅ, ᐱᔪᒥᓇᙱᑦᑐᖅ.
- ᑖᒃᑯᐊᓕ ᐃᓪᓕᖕᓂᑦ ᓄᖅᑲᖅᑎᑦᑎᓚᐅᙱᑦᑐᑦ.
- ᓰᖑᓂᐊᓘᕗᖅ ᐱᓂᕐᓗᖅᑲᑎᒌᖕᓂᖅ
  ᑭᓯᐊᓂᓕ ᑕᐃᒪᐃᓕᐅᖕᒋᓐᓇᓚᐅᖅᐳᑎᑦ.
  - ᐊᒃᓱᐃᓐᓂᖅ, ᓂᖕᖓᕐᓂᖅ, ᐊᑕᓂᐅᑉ ᒪᑭᒪᔾᔪᑎᖕᒋᑦ
    ᓴᖅᑭᑕᐅᓯᒪᔪᑦ ᒥᖕᓂᓂᕐᒧᑦ, ᐃᓄᐊᕐᓂᕐᒧᑦ,
    - ᐃᓛᔭᕐᓂᖅ!

ᐊᓄᕆᕐᔪᐊᖅ ᐊᒡᒋᖅᐳᖅ.
ᓯᕗᓕᑦᑕ ᓂᐱᖕᒋᑦ ᐃᔨᖅᓯᒪᕗᑦ.
ᐃᓯᔾᔪᒃᐳᑦ:
ᐅᓕᐸᑳᓕᕐᔪᐊᖅ ᑐᓗᒐᕐᓗ.
ᐸᐅᖅ ᐅᓪᓗᕆᐊᕐᓗ.
ᐊᕐᓇᖅ ᕿᒻᒥᓛᓪᓗ.
ᕿᒻᒥᖅ. ᖃᖁᓪᓗᒃ.
ᐱᔪᒪᔭᑦ ᖁᔭᓈᖅᑕᐅᔪᑦ
ᐊᑐᖅᓯᒪᔭᕐᓗ ᓯᖃᒃᑕᐅᔪᖅ.

Colonization of the vector:
- Intruder thing,
- you forgot something:
  your Honour, Obscene.
- Tyranny is unbecoming, unseemly.
- Yet that stoppered you none.
- It is a cruel thing to abuse one another
  but still you kept on.
  - Wealth, torture, the empire's fund
    built on greed, murder,
    - degradation!

A storm is coming.
Ancestral voices lurk.
They whisper:
Turtle and Raven.
Soot and Star.
Woman and Pups.
Dog. Fulmar.
Of dreams deferred
and the past marred.

ᑐᓃᑦ ᐅᑎᖅᑐᑦ

ᐊᖅᑯᓯᐅᕈᒃ ᑭᐳᖖᒐᔪᖅ.
ᐅᔭᒃᑭᑦ ᑎᑕᖅᑯᐃᑦ, ᓇᐸᔪᑯᑖᖅ ᐃᒡᓘ.
ᐊᑎᒍᒃ ᑲᒥᐊᓗᒃ ᐃᒡᓗᐊᓗ.
ᑕᕐᑐᕐᓂᖕᒋᑦ ᕐᑭᓗᖅᑭᓪᓗᒋᑦ.
ᒪᓕᖅᑲᑎᒌᓕᖅᑎᒃᑭᑦ.
ᑳᓇᓐ ᐅᑎᐊᓴᐅᑉ ᐊᓪᓗᕐᓂᖕᒋᑦ ᐃᓯᖅᑲᖖᒋᑦᑐᑦ
ᐃᑉᐱᒍᓯᖖᒋᑦᑐᒥᒃ ᓇᓕᖅᑯᑦᑕᖅᑐᖅ
ᐱᓂᕐᓗᒃᑕᖖᒋᑦᑐᖅ.

ᑐᑭᖅᑕᕈᑦ ᑐᐊᐸᒃ.
ᐃᑳᖅᑎᒃᑭᑦ ᐱᓐᓇᓂᔭᐅᔪᑦ.
ᓇᓕᒧᓕᖅᑎᒃᑭᑦ ᐅᓪᓗ ᐊᒻᒪᓗ ᐱᖅᑯᓯᑦ
ᐊᓂᖅᓴᐅᒪᔪᑦ ᐅᖅᑲᒻᒥᑕᒃᑐᓪᓗ ᑐᕌᕈᑎᒥ
ᑕᐅᕗᖓ ᕗᓇᓯᐅᑎᑦ ᒪᓕᒃᑐᕗᑦ.

ᐊᓯ, ᑭᓇᐅᖕᒪᖕᖔᑦ ᐊᐱᕆᖖᒋᓪᓗᒎ.
ᒪᓂᒪᑐᐃᓐᓇᔾᔮᖖᒋᑦᑐᒍᑦ
ᐊᖕᒐᒃ ᐃᓪᓗᐊᓂᒃ ᐅᐊᓴᕐᓗᓂ.

ᐱᖅᑯᓯᑦ ᑐᕐᑯᑕᐅᓂᖕᒋᑦ ᑲᑕᒃᑎᑦᑎᕗᑦ ᐊᑕᓂᓕᖕᓂᒃ.
ᐃᓗᐋᑦ ᓇᐸᔪᖕᒋᑦ ᐳᖅᑐᓯᕗᑦ ᓂᖅᑐᐃᓪᓗᑎᒃ
ᓯᓂᖅᑲᑎᑲᓪᒪᑦᑐᓂᒃ ᑖᐃᒪᓐᓂᒃ.

ᐊᑏᒎᖅ, ᓴᒡᓗᓯᕐᔭᐊᖅ.
ᑭᖕᒍᒧᑦ ᓴᐅᒥᖕᒧᓪᓗ ᓴᓂᒧᕐ!
ᐱᓯᒍᑎᒋᒍᒃ! ᐱᓚᐅᖖᒋᑦᑐᖅ ᓯᓕ.

Dorset Revenants

Plot the inverse.
Clear the corners, Rook.
One jackboot   then the other.
Work the angles.
Harmonize in procession.
Cannon Odessa's infinite steps with
indifferent precision
        and no consequence.

Kick gravel underfoot.
Bridge the values.
Balance the days and ways that
sigh and grumble crosshairs
                    down the motorcade.

Oh, do not ask who is it.
We will not be complicit
hands washing the Other.

Cultural assassinations de-spiritualize nations.
Headstones pile high to glorify
sleeping rough with diamonds.

Come now, great pretender.
        Back and to the left!
Walk it off!   It hasn't happened yet.

ᐃᓄᐃᓚᑦ ᐊᖏᕐᕋᕕᓃᑦ

ᐊᒃᓴᑳᔪᖅ, ᑎᑭᑦᑎᓇᓱᒃᑐᖅ ᐃᓗᒻᒧᑦ.
ᖃᓇᑦ ᐊᑎᓐᓃᑉᐳᑦ, ᑕᑦᑐᓐᓄᑦ ᑐᙵᕕᒃᑲ.
ᐊᑭᓯᕋ ᐃᒡᓘᑉ ᖄᖓᓂ, ᖁᖤᓃᑉᐳᑦ ᐊᑭᐊᓃᑦ
ᐃᕕᒃᓯᒪᑦ ᐅᐊᓱᓪᓗ,
ᑕᖤᓐᓂᒃ ᑲᐳᐃᔪᑦ.
        ᐱᕕᒃᐳᑦ ᐅᕙᓐᓂᒃ ᓄᖅᑲᖁᔨᔪᑦ.

ᖃᐃᓚᐅᕆᑦ, ᓇᕈᔩ.

ᓯᓗᑦ ᐃᓯᖤᑉᐳᑦ
ᐃᓴᕈᖏᑕ ᐊᑖᓂ.
ᓴᐅᓂᕕᓃᑦ ᐃᓱᔾᔪᒃᐳᑦ
ᐃᓚᖏᓐᓄᑦ ᐊᓯᐅᖅᑲᔪᓄᑦ.

ᐃᖅᓯᕗᖓ ᐅᒃᐱᖅᔪᐊᖅ ᓯᓐᓇᒃᑐᖅᑎᓪᓗᒍ
ᑲᑉᐱᐊᒋᕙᒃᑲᓗ ᐃᔨᐊᓗᖏᒃ
ᐃᖅᑑᒃ ᐃᓯᒫᓗᖕᓇᑎᒃ.

ᓂᖦᖤᙱᓪᓗᑎᒃ, ᓇᕈᔩ.
ᒫᓃᒋᐊᖅᑲᖅᐳᑎᑦ.

ᐃᒋᒃᑭᑦ ᓱᒃᑲᐃᑦᑐᑦ ᑑᕐᖓᑎᑦ, ᓴᒡᓗᔨᖅᔪᐊᖅ,
ᐃᓯᒐᖏᓐᓂᒃ ᐅᓂᐊᖅᐳᖅ ᐅᓐᓄᐊᒥ.
ᒥᓯᒪᔪᖅ ᐃᖦᖤᖅᑕ ᖃᓇᖏᓐᓂ,
ᒪᑭᖁᔨᖤᖅᑐᖅ.

Ghost Towns

Tumbling, reaching within.
Rafters below, tucked underneath my chin.
My rooftop pillow, my terraced echo
of straw and wire,
roots into my arms.
        Begs me to retire.

Come into my presence, pilgrim.

Feathers bristle
beneath Her wings.
Bone piles whisper
the kindred missing.

I cower behind Owl dreams
and dread their awful eyes
with indifferent screams.

Save your breath, wanderer.
You belongs here.

Dispense your slow ghosts, Deceiver,
shuffling through the night.
Perched upon our bedposts,
calling us to rise.

ᖃᐃᖁᔨᓚᐅᖅᐱᑕ ᐃᓕᖕᓂᒃ, ᓱᐴᒐᖅᑏ,
ᓲᕿᓯᓪᓗ ᑎᒃᓕᒐᕐᓗᒋᑦ?
ᑎᓪᓕᕐᓂᕐᒦᑦ ᒥᖅᑯᑎᒥᒃ ᓅᓯᒃᓯᓴᒥᒃ,
ᑕᑯᔭᐅᒃᑲᓐᓂᙱᑦᑐᒥᒃ?

ᑐᕌᖅᑎᑦᑎᐊᒃᑭᑦ ᐃᑉᐱᒍᓰᑎᑎᑦ, ᓇᓚᐅᑦᑖᖅᑎᕋᓛᖅ.
ᓴᙱᓃᑦ ᑲᑎᖅᓱᕈᒃ.
ᑕᕆᐅᖅ ᓂᑲᒋᙱᑦᓗᒍ, ᓇᔭᑯᓘᒃ.
ᖃᓂᓪᓕᓗᐊᖅᑕᐃᓕᒋᑦ.

Did we solicit thee, Piper,
to spirit the children?
From the pulse that pulls the needle,
ne'er to be seen again?

Calibrate your senses, little Sooth.
Muster your strength.
Be heavy handed with the salt, dear Sister.
Stay at arm's length.

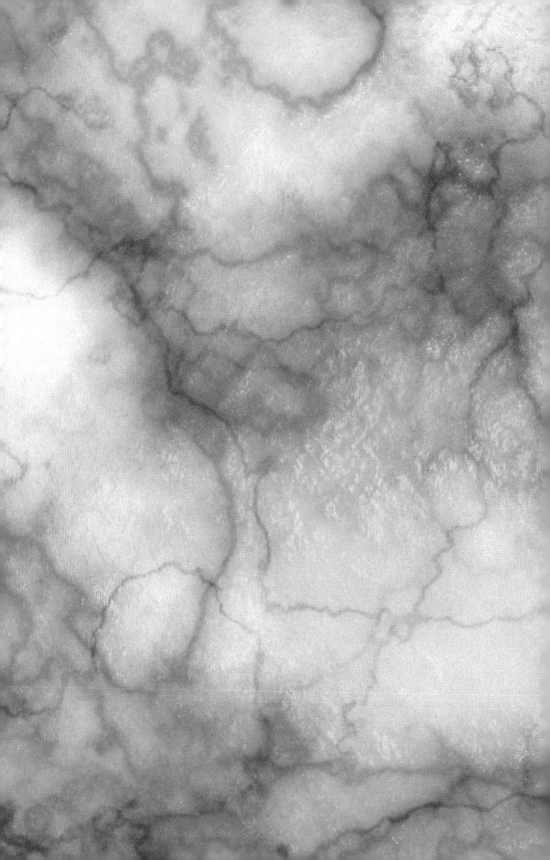

ᐅᕕᓂᒃ
Flesh

ᓯᓚᑖᓂ

ᓴᓂᖅ ᐃᓂᓪᓚᒍᓐᓇᙱᓚᖅ.
ᐊᑉᐸᖅᐸᓪᓕᐊᓂᖅ ᐊᖁᑕᐅᒍᓐᓃᖅᐳᖅ.
ᐊᓂᒍᖅᐸᓪᓕᐊᓂᖅ ᓅᖅᑲᑲᐃᓐᓇᖅᐳᖅ.
ᐅᓇ ᐊᕙᓗ ᓯᕿᖅᑕᐅᓯᒪᙱᑦᑐᖅ.

ᑭᓯᐊᓂᓕ, ᐅᖃᓕᒫᒐᕐᒥ ᓇᓗᓇᐃᒃᑯᑕᑦ ᓴᒡᓗᔪᓐᓇᙱᓚᑦ
ᑑᕐᖓᑦ ᖃᐅᒻᒪᓪᓛᑎᓪᓗᒋᑦ ᕿᒃᓯᒦᖅᑎᓪᓗᑎᑦ.

(ᐃᓴᖅᑯᐊᖅᑕᐅᓕᑦ)

ᑎᓇᒐᓂᐊᖅᐹᒃ, ᐱᓕᒻᒪᒃᓴᓇᑦ.
ᖂᖕᓃᑦ ᓅᙳᓪᓕ.
        ᑕᓇᐅᑉ ᐃᒪᖓ ᖃᐳᐊᖅᐳᖅ ᖃᓂᕐᒥ,
ᑕᓇᐅᖅ ᐃᓅᓯᕚᑦ ᐊᑭᖓ.

ᐃᓱᒃᑭᑦ ᑐᒥᑎᑦ.
ᑭᑭᐊᒃᑭᑦ ᐱᑐᖄᓗᐃᑦ ᑐᒥᑎᑦ
        ᒪᓂᕋᒧᕐ!
ᐱᕈᒃ ᑕᕐᕋᐃᕐ!
        ᑲᐅᒡᓕ ᐅᔭᕋᑦᑎᐊᖅ.

ᐃᕋᒃᑎᑦ ᐹᕐᖑᖅᐳᑦ ᓯᓚᒧ.
ᓂᐱᙵᑎᑦᑎᓂᖓ
        ᐅᑎᖅᑕᕋᐅᔭᙱᓚᖅ.
                ᑕᐃᒪᐃᑉᐸᓚᐅᕋᓗᐊᖅᐳᖅ.

Extraneous

Dust does not settle.
The descent is no longer controlled.
The moment is sustained.
This barrier unsoiled.

Yet, dog ears don't lie
while ghosts glimmer in the corner of your eye.

(Clip their wings)

Jackal, cut your teeth.
Slake your thirst.
        Seas foam at the mouth,
the salt of your worth.

Cover your tracks.
Nail your mistempered footprints
        to the ground!
Bury your shadow!
        Bring the hammer down.

The Howlers come crawling out.
The pull of their clout
        does not swing.
                Not like it used to.

ᖃᐅᔨᓂᐊᖅᑐᑦ ᐃᓕᓐᓂᒃ ᓇᐃᐱᑦᓯᓗᑎᒃ.
ᐹᕐᖑᖅᐳᑦ ᐃᓪᓗᒻᒧᑦ.
ᐃᓯᔾᔪᒃᐳᑦ ᓯᐅᑎᖕᓄᑦ
ᐅᖃᐅᑎᖃᖅᑐᑎᒃ ᐃᓗᖃᖖᒋᑦᑐᓂᒃ ᓇᓂᔭᖕᒋᓐᓂᒃ.

ᐅᒥᒃᓕᑦ ᐅᒃᑯᐊᑦ.
ᖅᑭᒫᒋᑦ ᐅᖅᑯᖅᒧᑦ, ᐊᓄᓇᖅᔭᐊᖅ ᐊᓂᒍᖅᓯᐊᓇᒍᒃ.
ᐱᑐᒋᑦ ᐊᖅᑰᑎᖅᒧᑦ.
ᑲᑭᐊᒃᑐᕈᖅ ᓯᖅᓗᐊᑉ ᒪᑐᖕᖓ.

They will find a way to you.
They will creep their way inside.
They will whisper in your ear
        of the hollowness they find.

Batten down the hatches.
Take shelter, weather the storm.
Bind yourself to the wheel.
Nail the cellar door.

ᑐᕙᖅᒥ

ᒪᐅᔭᓯᐅᖅᐳᑦ ᐅᓐᓄᓴᐅᑉ ᕿᒧᔾᔪᖏᓐᓂ.
ᒪᐅᔭᓯᐅᖅᑐᑦ ᓲᖅᑯᕐᒥᑎᒍᑦ.
ᐊᓄᕌᖅᑐᕐᒧᑦ ᖁᐊᖅᐳᖅ ᐅᑐᐊᖓ.

ᖁᖓᓯᕈᖅᑲᙱᑦᑐᖅ.

ᐊᑕᐅᓯᐊᑐᐃᓐᓇᐅᙱᓚᖅ ᐃᓪᓕᓂᓕᐅᖅᑐᑦ ᐅᓐᓄᒧᑦ
ᑖᒃᑯᓇᙵᑦ ᐊᖑᑎᓄᑦ ᑭᐱᙳᔪᓄᑦ ᐅᕙᓂᕈᖅᓯᒪᔪᓄᑦ.
ᐃᓪᓕᓂᓕᐅᖅᑐᑦ ᑕᐃᒃᑯᓄᖓ ᖄᔪᙱᑦᑐᓄᑦ
        ᑖᑉᓱᒥᖓ ᐃᒃᑮᖅᓇᖅᑐᒥᒃ,
                        ᑖᖅᑐᒥᒃ ᓄᓇᒥᒃ
        ᑲᒥᖃᑖᒃᓯᒪᔪᓄᑦ.

ᑕᐃᒃᑯᓄᖓ ᖃᑦᓲᓐᓇᖅᓄᑦ
ᐊᓂᖅᓵᖅᑕᐃᓕᒪᔪᓐᓇᖅᑐᓄᑦ ᐅᓐᓄᐊᒃᑯᑦ
ᖃᓂᐅᑉ ᐊᑯᓐᓂᐊᒍᑦ ᐅᔭᖅᑭᒐᔭᖅᑐᒥᒃ ᐃᓄᐃᓪᓚᖅᒥ
ᐅᓐᓄᓴᒃᑯᑦ ᑯᓂᒡᓗᒍ.

ᐃᒥᐊᑲᑕᒃᑐᑦ ᐃᓱᒪᕆᔭᑎᑦ,
ᑲᓪᓕᖅᐳᖅᓗ ᐊᑎᑦᑎᐊᖓᓂ,
ᐅᖃᐅᓯᓇᔭᑎᑦ ᓇᐃᑉᐳᑦ ᑐᕌᓪᓗᐊᖅᑐᑎᒡᓗ.
ᖁᐸᓄᐊᑯᓗᖕᒧᑦ ᑕᖃᐃᖅᓯᖅᑎᑕᐅᒐᔪᙱᑦᑐᑎᑦ.

ᐱᖃᑎᐊᓗᒃᑲ ᐱᕋᔭᐃᑦ
ᐊᑭᓕᖅᑕᐅᔪᒪᕗᑦ ᐱᑦᑎᐊᖅᑕᐅᙱᓐᓂᕐᒧᑦ.
ᕿᒫᓗᓂ ᓴᐅᓂᖅᑲᖅᕕᓐᓄᑦ
ᐱᐅᓛᖑᖅᑰᔫᙱᑦᑐᖅ.

Landfast

We trudged through evening drifts.
Down trodden paths knee deep.
Wind blown and teary cheeked.

Scarfless.

Not a one-off but a trail stomped into the night
by lonely men in shirtsleeves.
Clearing a path for those who'd brave
        those cold,
                        dark places
        with their small *kamiit.*

For those few who'd dare hold
their midnight breaths
between lips that would stone a patch of wilderness
with an evening kiss.

The thrumming of your thoughts,
thunder rumbles beneath,
your arguments terse and direct.
A hummingbird couldn't catch you breathe.

My cadre of ne'er-do-wells
demand their pound of flesh.
Defecting to my ossuary
leaves something to be desired.

kamiit (kah-MEET): Inuktitut term for three or more skin boots.

ᓄᓇᖅᐸᙱᖅ

ᐱᓯᕋ ᓱᕋᓕᖅᑐᖅ
ᐃᔾᔪᐊᖅᓯᒪᖅ ᐅᑭᐅᖅᑕᖅᑐᒥᐅᑎᑐᑦ.
ᓇᕝᕚᖅᐳᖅ ᐅᖃᕋᓱᒃᑕᒪ ᓄᖅᑲᖅᑕᕐᓂᖓᓂᒃ.
ᐊᖁᑉᐳᖅ ᒪᒥᐊᓐᓂᐊᓗᙱᑦ.

ᐊᓄᓇᑦ ᐅᖃᕐᓂᕐᓗᒃᐳᑦ
ᐱᖑᐃᑦ ᐃᑎᕖᙵᓐᓂᑦ.
ᑕᐅᕙᓂ ᒎᑎᐅᑉ ᕿᑐᕐᖓᓕᒫᙱᑦ
ᐃᓯᒐᐅᔭᖅᑖᖅᐸᒃᐳᑦ.

ᐃᑳᓇᑦ, ᑭᙲᒃᑭᒡᓗ ᑲᓱᒃᑎᒃᑭᑦ,
ᐊᓴᓂᖅ ᑲᐱᓯᒪᖅ ᐅᕖᓂᙳᑦ.
ᑕᐃᑲᓂᓗ ᑐᕌᕐᓂᙱᑦ ᕿᒥᙵᓂᐅᑉ ᓂᓪᓕᐊᓂᖓᑕ
ᓴᐅᓯᒪᒍᑦ ᐊᑖᓄᑦ.

ᒎᑎ ᐱᓂᕐᓗᒃᑎᐅᒪᖅ.
ᖁᑦᑎᒃᑐᖅ.
ᐅᓇ ᐃᓅᒪᖅ ᐊᑕᖅᑭᓂᕐᒧᑦ,
ᑕᐃᓐᓇ ᑕᐃᒪᐃᙶᑦᑐᖅ.
ᑖᒃᑯᐊᒃ ᐊᑕᓂᕐᔪᐊᖑᔫᔮᕈᓐᓇᖅᐹᒃ.
ᑖᒃᑯᐊᒃ ᓱᕋᑦᑎᓇᔪᓐᓇᖅᐹᒃ ᐳᖅᑐᔪᕐᒥᒃ ᐃᒡᓗᐊᓂ.

ᐱᙱᒐᕐᑲᑦᑕᖅᑐᑎᑦ ᐅᕙᓐᓂᒃ ᐊᑭᕋᙴᕐᓂᐊᕋᓱᒋᓪᓗᙱᒐ.
ᐃᓅᒃᑭᒃ ᖃᐅᒪᐅᔫᒃ
ᐅᕙᓐᓂᑦ ᐊᙱᕐᕋᕐᑯᐃᓕᖅᐹᒃ.

Anabasis

My degraded song
mimes hyperborean lilt.
Ekes out my stammer.
Rides my wild guilt.

Winds blaspheme
from the other side of the hills.
Where all God's children
got shoes.

Crossover, click your heels,
compromise tines skin deep.
Where ley lines of hate speech
bury underneath.

God is an unrighteous bastard.
Privileged.
This one born into honour,
that one   not so much.
Both may look at kings.
Both may tear His tower down.

You worry about me   going rogue.
Your lighthouse eyes
          beckon me home.

ᓂᐱᖏᑦ ᑕᓚᑎᑕᐅᓯᒪᔪᑦ ᖃᐃᓪᓚᒑᖅᐳᑦ
ᐊᕐᑭᑦᑐᖕᒐᓴᒃᑎᑦ ᓄᐊᑦᑎᖏᖅ ᐃᖕᕆᐅᓚᖕᓂᒃ.
ᒫᓂ ᒎᑎᖖᒍᐊᓛᒃ ᑕᕐᓂᑦ ᐃᓱᔅᔪᒃᐳᑦ
ᐱᖅᑯᓯᕐᒥᓂᒃ ᓱᐊᓛᑉ.

ᐊᓚᒃᑲᖖᕆᓐᓃᑦ ᑑᖅᑕᖅᑕᑦᑎᓐᓂᒃ ᑲᑦᑐᖅᑎᑦᑎᖏᖅ.
ᐊᓄᓇᖅᔪᐊᑦ ᓂᐸᐃᑦᑐᑦ ᑎᑭᑐᐃᓐᓇᓇᐊᖃᖅᐳᑦ.
ᕿᒪᒃᑕᐅᓂᑦᑎᓐᓂ, ᓴᐃᒪᓃᑦ ᕿᒃᓵᒍᑎᒋᓗᖏᑦ
ᒪᔪᓇᐊᖕᒐᓂ ᐱᖕᒎᑉ.

Our redacted voices ripple
joker mine waves.
Here idolatrous spirits whisper
mores of the Slave.

Your absence pulls our punches.
        Devoiced storms may rise.
In our loss, we mourn your peace
from the hillside.

ᐅᖕᒐᓯᒃᑐᑦ

ᓱᖕᒪᑦ ᐃᒪᐃᑉᐸ,
ᓂᑲᒍᓱᖕᓂᑦᑕ ᐃᑲᖅᖃᖕᒐᓂ,
ᐅᖅᑲᕈᓐᓇᐃᓪᓕᕙᒃᐱᑕ ᐃᑉᐱᒋᔭᑦᑎᓐᓂᒃ?
ᐅᖕᒐᕙᓇᐊᖅᑎᑦᑎᕙᒃᐳᒍᑦ, ᖁᔭᓈᖅᓯᕙᒃᐳᒍᑦ, ᓯᖁᑦᑎᓇᕙᒃᐳᒍ,
        ᐱᖖᒋᖖᒍᐊᖅᑎᑦᑎᕙᒃᐳᒍᑦ.

ᐆᒻᒪᑎᕗᑦ ᒥᖅᓱᖅᐳᖅ ᐅᕕᓂᕈᑦᑎᓐᓂᒃ
ᑲᑭᓂᓕᐅᑉ ᑐᓗᒐᐅᑉ ᐃᓴᕈᖕᒋᓐᓄᑦ ᐃᓂᓕᐅᖅᐳᖅ ᐊᑯᑦᑐᓯᕙᓪᓕᐊᔪᓂᒃ
ᑭᖖᒍᐊᖅᑐᖅ ᒥᑉᐳᖅ ᐆᒻᒪᑎᑦᑎᓐᓄᑦ
ᓄᒫᓱᖕᓇᖅᑐᖅ ᐃᖅᑲᐅᒪᔾᔪᑎ.

ᑕᓗᑉᑕ ᐃᓗᔅᑐᑦ ᑐᓄᐊᓂ
        ᑕᖅᖃᕗᑦ ᖅᑭᓄᕕᖅᑲᖅᐳᑦ.
ᓯᓚᑖ ᐅᓂᒃᑳᖅᑐᐊᑉ ᑲᓐᓄᔭᖅᒧᑦ ᖅᑯᓚᓯᒪᕗᖅ,
ᓲᖅᓇᖅᑐᑦ ᐱᕈᖅᐳᑦ, ᐳᐃᒍᖅᑕᐃᓕᖖᒐᓪᓗ ᖅᑭᓚᕈᑎᖖᒍᐊᑦ
ᑖᒃᑯᐊ
ᐃᖕᒍᓚᖅᓯᕗᑦ ᐊᖅᑭᐊᕈᑦᑕ ᐃᖅᑲᖕᒋᓐᓂᒃ
ᓲᖅᓗ ᑕᖅᖃᓕᑭᑖᑦ ᐊᓂᐅᖃᖅᐳᑦ ᖅᑲᓂᑦᑎᓐᓂᑦ
                ᑲᑕᒐᖅᓗᑎᒡᓗ ᐃᓗᐊᓂ
                ᓇᐹᖅᑐᖅᑲᖅᕕᐅᑉ.

Faraway

Why is it,
at the hour of our tenderness,
we find it impossible to say what we mean?
We defer, dismiss, dissolve,
        deny.

Our heart stitched shirtsleeves
tattoo Raven wing imprints widening as they carve
the alighted banks of our hearts
a forlorn souvenir.

Behind our folding wall screens
        our silhouettes plead.
While the exterior is gilded mythos,
cherry blossoms, and forget-me-knots
that
churn the pit of our stomachs
as butterflies escape our mouths
                to settle within
                the sylvan scene.

“ . . . ᐱᕈᖅᑐᑐᑦ ᒥᖁᓯᑑᑦ, ᐳᐃᒍᖅᐸᒃᐳᒍᑦ ᐸᖕᕕᖕᓇᖏᓐᓂᒃ
ᑲᒪᕿᖔᓚᖅᑐᑕ ᐱᑕᖃᕐᓂᐅᓂᖏᓐᓂᒃ.”

—ᒫᒡᒍᓇᑦ ᓗᐊᓇᓐᔅ

ᐊᔭᒍᑕᐅᑉ ᖁᓛᒍᑦ

ᐃᖁᒻᒪᕐᓂᐅᔮᓚᐅᖅᑐᖅ ᓯᓐᓇᒃᑐᑲᖕᒪᖕᓂᕐᒥᑦ,
ᐊᓄᓇᖅᔪᐊᖅ ᐃᑯᓪᓚᖅᑎᓪᓗᒍ,
    ᐊᒃᓱᕈᕐᓃᑦ ᐊᓂᒍᕐᓗᑎᒃ.
ᓯᕿᓂᖅ ᐊᑭᖕᒥᖕᓂᖓᓄᑦ ᓴᖅᑭᐸᐳᖅ ᓄᕗᔭᒃᑯᑦ,
    ᐱᕈᖅᑎᑦᑎᓪᓗᓂ ᐅᖃᐅᔭᓂᒃ.

ᑕᒃᓯᖅ ᓄᖑᓕᖅᐳᖅ   ᓴᔪᓗᓪᓗᓂ.
ᐃᕿᔪᖅ ᑕᖅᑯᒧᑦ.
ᑲᓚᐃᔅᑑᓯᐅᑉ ᑐᖁᑕᐅᓂᖓᓂᒃ ᐱᓪᓚᑦᑖᙳᐊᕐᓂᕗᑦ
ᐃᑳᖅᐳᖅ ᑕᑯᕐᓐᓈᕐᕕᐅᑉ ᓴᐅᒥᖓᓄᑦ.

    ᐃᓪᓚᖅᑏᑦ ᐃᓯᔾᔪᒃᐳᑦ.
    ᑐᐊᑦᑐᑦ ᑐᓗᒐᑦ ᐊᖅᑲᖅᐳᑦ ᓯᐅᑎᖕᓄᑦ.

ᓯᕿᓂᐅᑉ ᖃᐅᒪᓂᖓ ᓇᑎᕐᒥ ᐃᑳᖅᐸᓪᓕᐊᖅᔮᒃᐳᖅ.
ᐃᒐᑖᖅ ᓯᓂᓕᐅᖅᐳᖅ ᐅᑉᐱᕐᓂᕐᒥᒃ.
ᑕᖅᑐᑦ ᐃᖏᐅᓕᑦ ᐃᖏᕐᕋᕗᖅ ᖃᑯᖅᑕᐅᑉ ᖁᓛᒍᑦ.
ᐅᓐᓄᐊᖅᓯᐅᑎᑦ ᖁᐱᕐᕈᑦ ᐊᓂᖅᓴᐅᒥᕗᑦ ᖃᓯᒐᒥᒃ.

ᐃᖃᐅᒪᒋᑦ ᑲᑉᐱᐊᓇᖅᑐᒥᒃ,
ᓄᖅᑲᓇᑦ ᖃᐅᒪᓂᕐᒧᑦ.
    ᑕᖅᑭᖅ ᓄᖑᓕᖅᐳᖅ ᑖᕐᓂᕐᒧᑦ.
    ᓇᑲᕗᑦ ᓂᐅᖓᒃᐸᒃᑐᑦ ᐅᓐᓄᒃᑯᑦ.
    ᐅᕙᒍᓐᓇᔫᒐᓗᐊᖅᑐᑕ   ᓯᕗᒧᑉᐸᓪᓕᐊᕗᒍᑦ
    ᓇᒡᒍᐊᕐᓗᒃᐳᒍᑦ ᐅᓪᓗᓇᐊᑦ ᖃᐅᒪᓂᖏᓐᓄᑦ.

ᐃᓅᒃᑭᒃ ᐅᓚᓗᔮᒃ ᕿᓄᕘᒃ.
ᐅᒥᐊᖅᔪᐊᓄᑦ ᓄᓗᖅᐅᑎ ᐊᕙᓗᖓ ᓯᖁᑦᑎᓕᖅᐳᖅ.
ᖃᑭᔪᖅ ᐃᑎᔪᐊᓗᖕᒥᑦ, ᑖᓐᓇ ᐃᖃᓗᒃᔪᐊᖅ ᖁᕙᐅᖅᐳᖅ
ᑖᓐᓇᑑᒐᒥ ᐃᓕᒪᓱᒃᑐᓂᓗ.

". . . like the first dandelions, we would forget their weediness and marvel that they were there at all."

—Margaret Laurence

Over the Rainbow

It's like waking from a nightmare,
after the storm has passed,
          toils released.
The sun burns through the clouds,
          blossoming the leaves.

The mists part   and quiver.
Curl into shade.
The curtain call of our Passion play
crosses from stage left.

          Hyenas whisper.
          Narrow ravens coo in your ear.

Sunlight inches across the floor.
Window frames belief.
Dark waves roll over white.
Crickets sigh relief.

Recall in terror,
balk at the light.
          The Moon wanes into darkness.
          Our stalks bend in the night.
          Despite ourselves   we advance
          gnarled by starlight.

Your hurricane eyes plead.
The lighthouse mortar caves.
Rising from the Deeps, this leviathan weeps
alone and afraid.

ᐃᓄᐃᓚᑦ

ᓯᖅᓈᖅᑎ ᓱᑲᖓᕗᖅ.
ᓴᓐᕙᖕᒧᑦ ᑕᓚᖖᒐᑎᑦᑎᕗᖅ.
ᐅᖅᑲᒻᒥᓃᑦ ᐃᔨᖅᓯᓯᒪᕗᑦ ᐱᒋᐊᖅᓂᖏᓐᓂᒃ.
ᐊᓄᓇᒧᑦ ᖃᐃᖅᑲᒃᓯᒪᔪᖅ ᓱᓚᔪᖅᓇᖅᓇᓂᓗ.

ᑐᑭᓯᓇᐃᓐᓇᖅᑎᒍᒃ, ᐊᖅᑭᑦᑐᖓᔫᖅ.

ᑕᕝᕙᐅᕗᖅ ᐃᓅᓰᑦ ᕿᓚᒃᓱᐃᔪᖅ
ᐊᑕᐅᓯᐅᓈᖅᑎᖅᑐᒥᑦ ᓂᒃᓱᒃᑕᖅᓂᖏᑦ.

ᐃᓯᕙᑦᑐᖅ,
ᓄᑮᑦ ᓱᖏᐅᑎᓯᒪᓂᖏᑦ ᐃᖅᑲᐅᒪᕗᑦ
ᒪᓐᓇ ᕿᔪᒃᑖᕈᓗᒃ
ᑐᐱᐅᑎᒋᕙᖃ ᐃᓐᒋᐊᓐᓂ.
ᖃᒃᑭᓐᓇᖅᑐᖅ, ᕿᖅᓗᑎᔪᖅ.
ᑕᖅᑭᐅᑉ ᐅᐊᑦᑎᔮᐊ
ᒥᐊᓐᒎᖅᐳᖅ ᓇᓗᓕᐅᖅᑲᔪᖅ.

ᐅᐃᓇᓴᖅᑐᖅ ᐃᑯᒫᓘᑉ ᐅᒃᑯᐊᖓᓂ,
ᐃᑦᑐᖖᒍᖅᐳᖓ
ᑮᖏᖅᓯᓇᓱᒃᑐᖓ.

ᑕᕝᕙᐅᕗᖅ ᐃᓅᓰᑦ ᐃᓯᕙᓕᖅᑐᖅ
ᐊᑕᐅᓯᐅᓈᖅᑎᖅᑐᓂ ᓄᕙᖅᓴᖅᓯᒪᓂᖓ.

ᑐᑭᓯᐊᖖᒋᑦᑐᖅ, ᑐᑭᓯᓇᑦᑎᐊᖖᒋᑦᑐᖅ, ᑲᖖᒍᓇᖅᑐᓂᒃ ᐅᖅᑲᖅᑐᖅ.
ᑎᒃᑕᐅᖃᓛᒃᑐᖅ ᐅᖅᑲᖓ ᑖᖅᑐᒥ.
ᓲᐸᒐᖅᑐᖅ ᑕᑯᒃᓴᐅᖖᒋᑦᑐᖅ.

ᑖᖅᑐᐊᓗᐃᑦ ᐃᖏᐅᓚᒃᐳᑦ ᕿᓐᓂᖅᑕᑦ.
ᑎᓂᓚᖅᓂᐅᑉ ᒥᓗᖕᓂᖓ ᐅᑎᖅᐳᖅ.
ᐃᖅᑲᖅᓗ ᐃᒪᖅᒧᑦ ᐅᓚᑉᐳᖅ,
ᑕᐃᑲᓂ ᐃᓗᓐᓄᑦ ᓇᓗᓇᐃᓚᐅᖅᓂᕗᑦ ᑲᑕᖕᓂᖓᓂ.

Hinterlands

Tense knitter.
Close to the chest.
Cleverly veiled assails.
Wind-chafed and suspect.

Keep it simple, stupid.

This is your life   binding
one loop at a time.

Uncoiled,
muscle memory remembers
this blasted heath
malingering in the throat of me.
Tannic,   constricted.
The Moon's sentinel
howls conflicted.

Courting Hell-gate,
        I grow old
        turning the key.

This is your life   unravelling
        one line at a time.

Obtuse, obscure, obscene.
Flutter-tongue in the dark.
        Embouchure unseen.

The dark storming waves of black.
The draw of tides blown back.
Devoured beneath the waves,
where we reached out   collapsed.

ᓴᙱᒌᑦᑐᑦ

ᑲᑭᓪᓚᕐᓇᑦ ᐃᕕᒃᓯᒐᐃᓪᓗ ᑐᕐᕈᔪᑦ ᑲᑭᔭᑉᐳᑦ
ᓴᐅᓂᑯᓗᒃᑎᓐᓄᑦ ᓇᑲᓴᕋᐃᑦᑐᓄᑦ.
ᐃᑉᐱᒍᓱᓗᐊᕋᑦᑕ ᐱᐅᙱᓐᓂᑦᑎᓐᓂᒃ
ᖁᔭᓈᖅᓯᔭᕆᐊᖓ ᐃᓱᖏᓐᓂᒃ ᐅᖃᖅᑕᐅᔫᑦ.

ᕿᒃᓵᖕᓂᖅ ᐃᐱᒃᐳᖅ
ᐅᕙᑦᑎᓐᓄᑦ ᑑᕐᖓᕐᓄᑦ ᐊᖏᕐᕋᖅᑲᙱᑦᑐᓄᑦ.
ᖃᐅᒪᓂᖅᑲᙱᑦᑐᖅ,
ᐊᓕᐊᓇᕐᓂᕐᒥᒃ ᐱᙱᙵᐊᖅᑎᑦᑎᔪᖅ.

ᖁᐸᓄᐊᑦ ᑎᖏᒪᕗᑦ ᖁᓛᒍᑦ ᐃᕕᒃᓯᒐᐃᑦ
ᐳᖅᑐᓂᑯᓘᑦ ᓴᒡᕕᑦᑎᓐᓄᑦ ᑎᑭᐅᒪᕗᑦ. ᑎᒃᑕᐅᕋᓛᖅᐳᑦ
ᐃᕕᒃᓯᒐᑦ ᐆᔭᐅᔭᑦ ᐱᕈᖅᑐᑦ. ᓂᐸᐃᑦᑐᖅ ᐃᒪᕕᒃ
ᐃᖏᐅᓕᒃᐳᖅ.

ᒥᓱᐸᒃᐳᑦ ᐃᒪᕐᓄᑦ ᐃᒃᑲᒃᑐᓄᑦ
ᓄᙳᓴᖅᑐᓄᑦ ᓯᕐᑭᓂᕐᒥ.
ᐃᒡᓗᓕᐅᓇᐊᖅᑐᖅᑐᑦ ᐃᓚᒌᓄᑦ ᐊᖏᕐᕋᐅᓂᐊᖅᑐᓂᒃ.
ᐸᖅᑭᑦᑎᐊᕐᓂᐊᕐᒪᑕᓗ ᕿᑐᕐᖓᖏᓐᓂᒃ.

ᑐᓗᒐᑦ ᕿᓗᒃᐳᑦ ᑭᔅᓯᖅᑐᒥ.
ᐃᓴᐅᔫᑦ ᐅᑭᐅᖅᓯᐅᑎᖏᓐᓂᒃ.
ᑐᓴᖅᐳᑦ ᕿᑭᕐᕌᕐᓂᓐᓂᒃ,
ᓈᓚᒃᐳᓪᓗ ᖃᑭᐊᓕᕐᓂᓐᓂᒃ.

ᑐᙳᔪᐊᖓᔪᑦ, ᓄᓇᕋᑦ
ᓯᓂᓕᐅᖅᐳᑦ ᐃᓪᓕᓂᕐᒥᒃ.
ᓄᓇᕋᖕᒋᑦ ᓂᕈᔭᐅᔫᒃᓴᐅᕗᑦ,
ᓴᙱᔫᑦ ᐸᖅᑭᕗᑦ ᓴᙱᒌᑦᑐᓂᒃ.

Frail

Burs and foxtails stick
to our brittle little bones.
Too mindful are we of our flaws
to forgo conclusions.

Megrims barb
to we vagrant dead.
          Devoid of light,
denying the dread.

Swallows glide o'er wheatgrass
as high as our chest. Rippling
fields of greenery. A silent ocean
crests.

They dive to sparse puddles
drying in the sun.
To build a home for their family.
To protect their young.

The Ravens bark in the heat.
Moulting winter skins.
They harken my footfalls,
hear my confessions.

In fiery purples, clover
shepherds the trail.
Their flowers are to be eaten,
          the strong protects the frail.

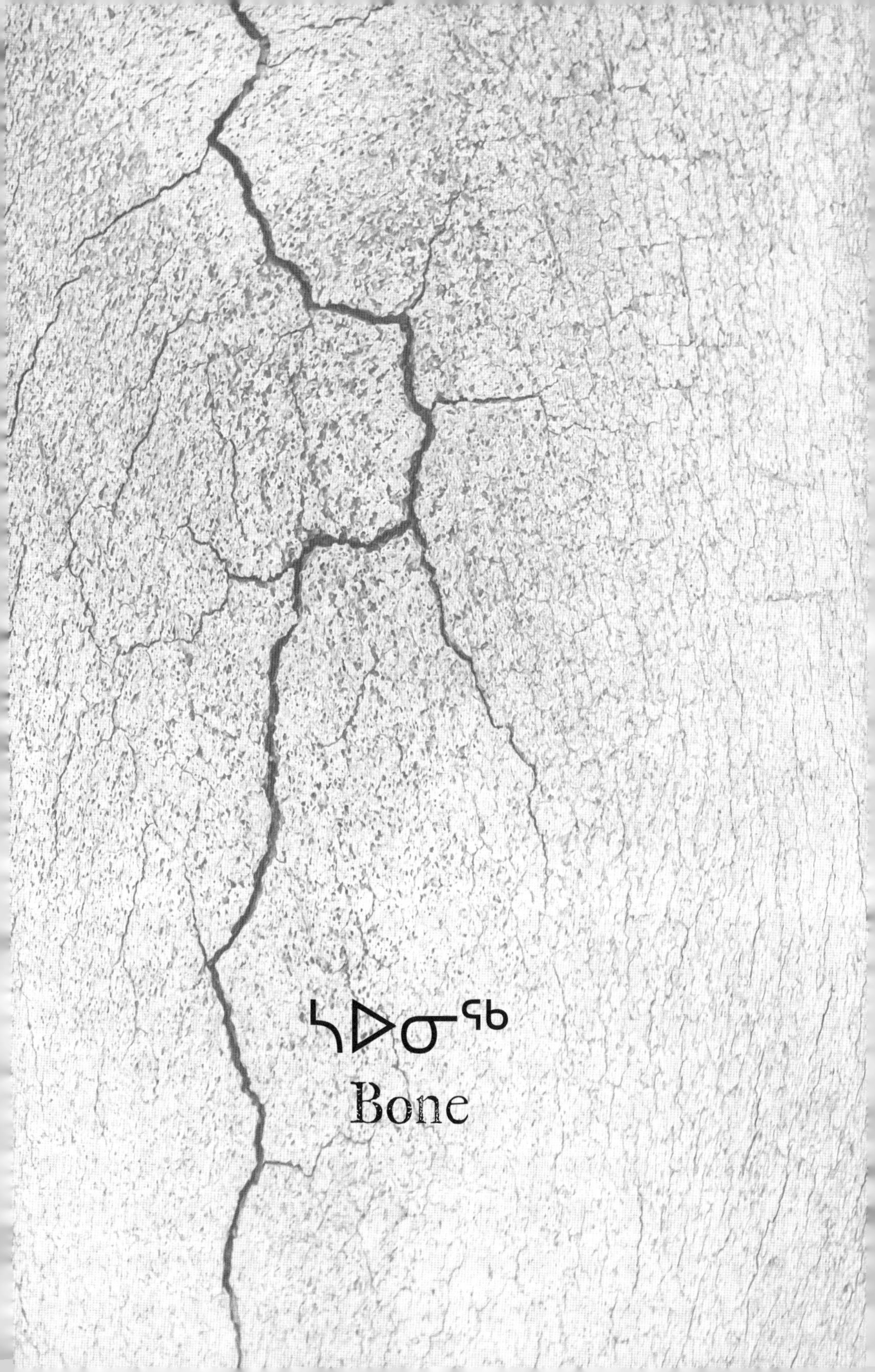

ᓴᐅᓂᖅ
Bone

ᐃᓄᐊᖅᑕᐅᓕᑦ ᐅᓪᓗᕆᐊᑦ

ᑐᕐᑯᕋᐃᕕᖓᓂ ᓯᓐᓇᒃᑐᓂᒃ.
ᐱᓚᒃᑐᖅᑕᐅᔪᑦ
ᓴᖅᑭᓯᒪᕗᑦ ᓇᒡᓕᖕᓂᕐᒥᒃ ᐊᓯᐅᔾᔨᓯᒪᓂᕗᑦ.
ᑖᒃᑯᐊ ᓇᓕᒧᒌᙱᐸᐳᑦ, ᐋᓐᓂᖅᓯᔪᑦ ᐃᑭᓕᖅᓯᔪᑦ
ᑕᐃᑲᙵᑦ ᐋᓐᓂᖅᓇᖅᑐᓂᒃ ᐃᖅᑲᐅᒪᓂᕐᒥᒃ.
ᐃᕐᕈᕐᕕᒃ.
ᓄᖑᓴᖅᑕᐅᔪᖅ. ᓄᖑᑦᑐᖅ.
ᐱᑕᖅᑲᕈᓐᓃᖅᑐᖅ.
ᓱᕈᓕᑭᐊᙳᖅᑐᖅ.

ᐅᓇᑕᐅᑎᕗᑦ ᐃᓕᐅᖅᑲᓚᐅᖅᐸᕗᑦ
ᐅᕐᕈᐃᓐᓇᖅᐳᒍᓪᓗ ᒪᕐᕋᕐᒧᑦ ᐊᓯᑦᑎᓐᓄᑦ
ᐃᓯᒐᖏᓐᓂᒃ ᒪᕐᓇᑎᑦᑎᒐᓴᙱᑦᑐᒧᑦ ᓱᕈᕐᒧᑦ.
ᐊᒡᒐᕗᑦ ᐊᐅᕐᒋᓐᓇᕈᓚᐅᖅᐳᑦ ᒪᑭᒪᖅᑲᑎᒌᒐᓱᒃᑐᑕ.
ᑕᒻᒪᓚᐅᖅᐳᒍ, ᑕᒻᒪᙱᕐᕋᑕᓗ.
ᐊᓯᕗᑦ ᐋᒃᑳᓚᐅᖅᐳᑦ.
ᑭᓯᐊᓂᓕ ᐅᑯᖓᓚᐅᖅᐳᒍᑦ ᐊᒡᒍᕋᖅᑐᑕ ᐊᓄᕆᕐᒥ ᐃᑯᓪᓚᔪᐃᑦᑐᒥ.
ᐃᓗᑖᓴᖅᑕᐅᓚᐅᖅᐳᒍᑦ ᐅᐊᓴᖅᑐᑕᓗ ᖃᐅᒪᓂᑦᑎᓐᓂ.
ᐊᒻᒪᓗ, ᑎᑕᒃᑐᖅ ᐱᐊᓂᖕᒪᑦ,
ᐃᒃᓯᕙᐅᑕᓪᓗ ᑭᐳᓄᑦ ᐊᕝᕙᐃᖅᑕᐅᓪᓗᑎᒃ.
ᑎᒍᒻᒥᖅᑲᑎᒌᓚᐅᖅᐳᒍᑦ
ᑕᕝᕙᑐᐊᖑᖅᑲᑎᒌᒃᑲᑦᑕ ᓵᕝᕕᒃᓴᖅᑲᒃᑲᓐᓂᖅᓇᑕ.

ᑕᕝᕙᑐᐊᑦ ᐱᔪᒪᓚᐅᖅᐸᕗᑦ.

ᑕᐃᒫᒃ, ᐃᓯᕆᑦ ᐃᓕᒌᒃᑯᓐᓄᑦ.
ᐃᓂᓪᓚᒃᓴᐃᓚᐅᖅᑕ ᐃᓪᓕᕆᓂᐊᖅᑕᕐᓂᒃ.
ᑖᒃᑯᐊ ᓴᓇᓯᒪᕙᕗᑦ
ᓴᓇᑲᒻᒪᒃᓯᒪᔪᐊᓗᐃᑦ.

Murder the Stars

In the abattoir of dreams.
The processed scraps
        that stem from our love lost.
The pieces that do not fit,   that hurt and wound
from that painful place beyond memory.
The fount.
Erased.   Gone.
Null.
        Moot.

We laid our weapons down and
slumped in the dirt when Others
would not sully their feet in the base clay.
We bloodied our hands holding each other up.
        We were wrong, but not really.
Others had said no.
Yet we bent under constant winds.
Hollow and bathed in each other's light.
        And, when the music was over,
        and the chairs put on the tables.
        We held onto each other
        because that was all we had.

        That was all we needed.

So, come in if we be friends.
        Let us make you a bed.
This is our design
                flawed to no end.

ᒪᓕᖕᓂᖅ

ᐱᑕᖃᕐᓂᓕᒫᖅ ᓯᓚᕐᔪᐊᕐᒥ
ᓯᕗᓂᖅᐳᖅ ᐊᓕᒍᖅᑎᑐᑦ.
    ᐊᒃᓱᕈᓈᖅ ᐃᑳᕈᑦ ᐅᐊᔭᐅᒐᖅ ᐃᐱᒃᑐᖅ
ᖃᓕᒍᑳᖅᐳᖅ ᖃᑕᐃᑦᑐᒥᒃ.
ᓂᐸᐃᑦᑐᑦ ᐃᖁᖕᓃᑦ.
ᑲᓐᓄᔭᖅᓯᓐᓂᑦᑐᖅ
ᑲᐃᓪᒥᐅᑎᒎᑦ ᐅᖃᐅᓯᖅᓂᒃ ᖃᓂᓐᓄᑦ.
    ᖃᓗᖁᖅᐳᖅ ᓂᐱᓂᒃ ᑕᑯᒃᓴᐅᙱᑦᑐᓂᒃ.
ᐱᔪᒥᓇᖅᐳᖅ. ᐃᒃᓴᓇᖅᐳᖅ.   ᑕᐃᓐᓇ ᖁᖓᑦᑐᖅ ᐅᖃᓪᓚᙳᐊᖅᑎᑦᑎ
ᐃᓱᔾᔪᒃᐳᖅ ᐱᔪᓐᓇᙱᓐᓂᓐᓂᒃ.
ᐃᒃᓴᒍᖕᓂᕐᒥᒃ ᖃᑦᑎᖅᓯᒐᖅ.

ᑖᒪᓂ, ᐊᐅᓚᑦᑎᔪᓐᓇᕐᓂᖅᑲᖅᐳᖓ. ᓄᕿᑦᑎᔪᓐᓇᖅᐳᖓ. ᓲᖑᓂᖅᑲᖅᐳᖓ
    ᐆᒪ ᓇᐹᖅᑐᖅᑲᖅᕕᐅᑉ ᓯᓚᑖᓂ
ᐱᕈᖅᓯᐊᒃᓴᐅᒐᖓ ᐊᓄᓇᒥ ᑎᒃᑕᐅᔪᖓ.
ᐅᖃᐅᔭᖅ ᐳᒃᑕᒐᖅ ᑖᖅᑐᒥ ᑰᖕᒥ
ᑰᒃᑐᒥ ᐊᖕᒋᖅᓱᒧᑦ.
ᐱᑐᐃᔅᓴᓇᐊᖅᑐᖅᑐᖅ
ᓯᖄᖅᑐᒥᒃ   ᓂᐱᐊᓗᖕᒥᒃ.

ᐅᓇ ᑕᕝᕙ ᐃᓅᓰᑦ   ᐃᐱᒃᓴᖅᑐᖅ
ᐊᑕᐅᓯᐅᓈᖅᑐᒋᑦ ᐹᓇᖕᒋᑦ.

ᖁᐱᙳᓚᔪᖅ ᓴᕝᕋᔭᒃ,
ᖁᑦᑐᒃᐳᖅ ᐃᖏᐊᖕᓚᓄᑦ ᐅᐃᔾᔭᓪᓛᔫᑉ.
ᑐᓵᙱᑦᑐᖅ ᐊᑕᓂᐅᕙᖅᑲᖅᕙᖓᓂᒃ,
ᐊᑕᓂᒎᑦ ᓱᖁᒃᓯᒪᔪᖅ   ᐅᐃᓪᒪᐅᖅᑲᒐᖅ.

ᑕᕐᓂᖅ ᐃᒪᐃᖅᐳᖅ,
ᐃᓅᓯᐅᑉ ᕿᐃᓂᖕᒪᓂᒃ ᐅᕿᓐᓂᑦ.
ᓂᐅᕝᕕᐅᕆᐊᖅᑎ ᑐᖅᑯ ᐃᓪᓚᖅᐳᖅ ᑭᒍᑎᒪ ᐅᖓᑖᓂᑦ.

ᑲᓪᓕᖅᐳᖅ ᐊᒻᒪ   ᒪᓪᓕᖅᐳᖅᓗ ᓯᓪᔭᒧᑦ.
ᐅᓇ ᐅᐊᑦᑎᕆ ᓴᒃᑯᐃᔭᐅᔪᓐᓇᖅᐳᖅ,
ᑕᐃᒪᐃᒍᓐᓇᕈᓂ—ᓴᐃᓪᒪᖅᓴᖅᑕᐅᔪᓐᓇᑐᐃᓐᓇᖅᐳᖅ.

Pilgrimage

All of existence
ringing like a glass.
          Tightrope razor wire
seething to a shrill.
Silent screams.
The taste of copper
heaves words into my mouth.
          Dredges voices unseen.
Enticing. Alluring.   That smiling ventriloquist
whispers my weakness.
Smoulders desire.

Here, I may hold sway.   Pull.   Clout.
          Outside these woods
I am a seed on the wind.
A leaf on dark rivers riding
the flow tide home.
To unleash
white   noise.

This is your life   honing
one edge at a time.

Metal twisting,
scratching down the jaws of spirals.
Deaf to his kingdom,
our broken King   shambles on.

Soul tapped,
the wine of life flowing out of me.
The Harbinger laughs   behind my teeth.

A peal of thunder and   a crash of waves.
This sentinel can be discharged,
if at all—only allayed.

ᓯᓐᓇᒃᑐᕐᓂᕐᓗᖕᓂᖅ ᒫᓐᓇ ᐱᔪᖅ

ᕿᒃᓵᒍᑎ ᐱᓯᖅ ᐊᓂᒍᐃᔪᓄᑦ.
ᐃᖏᕐᓂᖅ ᐃᑎᓂᖅᐹᕐᒧᑦ ᓇᓗᓇᐃᒃᑯᑕᓂᒃ
ᑕᐃᑲᓂ ᑲᑐᔾᔨᓚᐅᖅᐳᑦ ᐱᕕᓕᖅᑐᑕ
ᑲᑦᑐᖅᑎᑉᐹᑎᒍᓪᓗ ᐃᓱᓕᓐᓂᑦᑕ.

ᐃᓱᒫᓗᓗᐊᙱᑦᑐᑦ ᓴᓇᔾᔪᑦ ᐱᐊᓂᙱᒃᑲᓗᐊᖅᐸᑕ
ᐃᓱᒪᓂᖅᓴᐅᕗᓪᓕ ᐱᓇᓱᐊᕐᓂᕐᒥᒃ.
ᐊᖕᖑᐃᓇᐊᕐᓗᓂ. ᐱᓕᖅᑐᑦ ᐃᖏᐅᓕᒃᐳᑦ.
ᓯᓚᕐᔪᐊᓕᐅᕈᓐᓇᕐᑯᓪᓗᒍ.
ᑲᖏᖑᐅᔾᔨᓂᖅ ᐱᔮᓇᒃᐸᑦ
ᐱᐅᓂᖅᓴᐅᕗᖅ.

ᐅᓇ ᓯᓐᓇᒃᑐᕐᓂᕐᓗᒃᐳᖅ ᐋᓯᑦ.
ᐅᓂᒃᑳᖅᑕᐅᔪᖅ ᐱᐊᓂᒃᑎᑦᓗᒍ, ᐱᑐᐃᔾᔮᓰᖑᕗᖅ.
ᐃᑳᑲᑕᒃᑐᖅ ᐃᓱᖅᑲᙱᑦᑐᒧᑦ.

ᑕᒪᓐᓇ ᐱᓕᕆᔾᔪᑎᓄᑦ ᐱᖅᑯᓯᖅ
ᐅᒃᑯᓯᖕᓃᑦᑐᑦ ᐃᒐᕕᖕᓂ
ᓴᓇᓂᐅᕗᖅ ᓇᓪᓚᐅᓐᓂᖅᓯᐅᕐᓂᕐᒥᒃ ᓯᓚᕐᔪᐊᑉ ᐃᕐᖓᐅᑎᖕᖓᓂ.
ᑕᐃᑲᓂ ᐅᖅᑯᒃᓴᐅᓯᓇᐅᔨᐅᔪᒧᑦ,
ᑑᕐᖓᐅᔪᒧᑦ,
ᐅᑕᖅᑭᕗᒧᑦ. ᐅᐊᑦᑎᕗᒍ.
ᐃᔨᐊᓗᒃᐳᑦ ᑮᓇᐅᔭᐅᔮᖅᑐᑦ ᓴᕕᕐᔭᑦ
ᒪᕐᑯᓕᕐᑯᓪᓗᒍ ᑐᒃᓯᐊᖅᐳᑦ.

A Nightmare in Progress

A swan song dirge.
A chant of high-water marks
where we pooled our last ditch
        and caught our limit.

        They do not care for the finished product
                but the gesture.
        To go out of the way.   Consequence wave.
        To make time and space.
                The more personal the delay
                the better.

He's having nightmares again.
When the story's over, he's set free.
Cross over   infinitely.

This mechanical behaviour
in the cauldron of kitchens
forges ceremony in the grease trap of the universe.
Where we boilermen,
we bogeymen,
are waiting.   Watching.
Our silver-dollar eyes
pray for rain.

“ᐃᑯᐊᓚᔪᖕᒐ, ᐆᑎᑉᐸᕆᑦ—ᐃᓕᓐᓂᒃ ᐃᑭᑦᑎᓪᓗᖕᒐ, ᐃᑯᐊᓪᓚᑦᑎᐊᖅᐳᖕᒐ, ᐃᑯᐊᓚ
ᐆᓇᖅᐳᖅ ᖃᐅᒪᑦᑎᐊᖅᑐᓂᓗ ᐊᑭᒻᒥᖕᒪᓇᒃᐳᖅ ᑕᑯᒥᓇᖅᑐᓂᓗ.”

—ᑯᕿᐃᖅ ᒥᐊᓗ

ᓯᓚᐃᕐᓇᓯᔾᔪᑎᑦ

ᓂᐱᓗᒃᐳᖅ ᐃᓪᓚᖅᑐᖅ,
ᐃᔨᖕᕆᒃ ᕿᕕᐊᖅᓴᓪᓛᕗᒃ ᕿᒦᒃᑐᑎᒃ.
ᐃᔨᕈᓐᓇᖅᐳᖅ ᐃᓕᒪᓯᓕᕈᓂ.
ᐅᖃᐅᑎᓇᓱᖖᒐ ᑕᓛᓃᖖᕆᓐᓂᖕᒐᓂᒃ ᑕᓛᓃᓚᐅᖖᕆᓐᓂᖕᒐᓂᒃ.
ᐃᓱᓛᓗᓇᖖᕆᑦᑐᖅ, ᓴᐃᓕᔪᓐᓇᖅᐳᑎᑦ.

ᒪᓐᓇ ᐱᔪᓐᓇᖅᑕᐃᑦ.

ᓚᐃᔭᓐ ᐃᔭᖅᓯᒪᕗᖅ ᐃᕕᒃᓱᒐᑰᒥ.
ᑯᑉᐳᐃᑦᑐᖅ ᕿᓖᕗᖅ ᖃᐃᕈᓯᖕᒐᓄᑦ.
ᐅᑕᖅᑭᔪᖅ. ᐅᑕᖅᑭᐅᓴᐃᓐᓇᖅᑐᖅ.
ᐃᖅᓯᓇᖅᑐᓄᑦ ᕿᒪᒃᑕᐅᒃᓯᖅᑐᑦ. ᐊᒃᓯᕈᕐᓇᖅᓯᑎᓪᓗᒍ.
ᐅᕝᕙᓗ ᐃᒫᒃ ᐊᓂᔪᓐᓇᖅᓯᒃᐸᑦ ᐊᓂᔪᓐᓇᖅᓯᒃᐸᑦ.
ᑐᓂᕐᕈᓯᐊᖅ ᖃᖕᒐᓕᒫᓄᑦ. ᑐᓂᕐᕈᓯᐊᖅ ᓄᖑᒍᓐᓇᖖᕆᑦᑐᖅ.
ᐅᓇ ᐃᕐᖑᓯᖅ ᐃᒥᖖᕇᓐᓇᕈᓐᓇᖅᐸᕿ
ᓱᓕ ᐅᓇ ᓱᑲᑦᑕᓪᓛᓂᖅ ᑕᐃᒪᐃᖕᒋᓐᓇᕐᓂᐊᖅᑐᖅ
ᐃᔫᑦ ᐅᖕᒐᑖᓂ
ᒥᑕᐅᑎᔪᖅ ᖁᖕᒐᑦᑐᖅ ᑕᐃᒪᐃᖁᔾᑯᖅ,

ᑐᖁᑦᑎᔪᓐᓇᖅᐱᑦ ᐱᑕᖃᖖᕆᑦᑐᒥᒃ?

ᓄᓇᖅᑲᑎᒌᓪᔪᐊᑦ ᐅᕙᓐᓂᒃ ᖃᐃᖁᔾᔭᓕᖀᖕᒐᑕ,
ᐊᖕᒋᖅᑲᓐᖓᖕᒋᑕᒥ ᓇᔪᖅᑐᑦ ᐃᓗᕕᖅᑲᖅᕕᒃᑐᑦ
ᒥᑕᐅᑎᖅᑲᕈᒪᓂᖕᒐ ᓄᔭᖕᒋᓐᓂ ᓂᒐᕕᓯᒪᔪᖅ.
ᐊᓪᒐᖕᒋᑕ ᐃᕿᑦᑕᕐᓂᖕᒋᑦ ᓯᖅᑲᓕᓄᑦ ᓯᓚᐃᕐᓇᓯᔾᔪᑎᑦᑎᒋᐅᕙᐃᑦ
ᕿᓪᓕᖅᐳᓪᓘᓐᓃᑦ ᖃᐅᒪᓪᓛᔪᑦ.
ᐊᓯᕈᐃᑯᕐᓗ ᒨᓗᒥᒃ ᓅᓛᓯᖕᓂᕐᒎᑦ.

"Smoldering, I burn you—burning you, I flare,
Hot and bright and fierce and beautiful."
—*Frank Miller*

Artifice

Rasping chuckles,
eyes dance with malice.
He can hide when threatened.
Convince me he's not there and never was.
        There's no need to worry,   to fret.

        You got this.

A lion in tall grass.
A bear retreating to his cave.
Waiting.   *Always waiting.*
For when the coast is clear.   When the chips are down.
Or when it's   *green light*   *green light.*
A gift for all occasions.   The gift that keeps on giving.
I can deny this cup at my lips
yet   this twitch will remain
behind the eyes
a mocking smile insists,

        Can you kill what does not exist?

When the city calls out to me,
squatting like a graveyard
        with mischief in her hair.
Her knuckle coin tricks
or glittering flecks
transmutes gold to despair.

ᐅᕗᖖᒐᐅᑎᖃᑦᑕᖅᑖᖕᒐ ᓴᖖᕇᓪᓕᒑᖕᒐᒪ.
ᐅᕿᔮᕙᒃᐳᒧᒃ ᓄᓕᐊᖅᑐᑐᑦ.
ᐊᔾᔨᒋᓕᖅᑐᒍ ᑕᐃᓐᓇ ᖁᖕᒐᓐᓂᕐᓗᖕᓂᖅ. ᐱᕙᒃᐹᖕᒐ
ᐃᓅᕕᐊᑐᖃᖅᑎᑐᑦ
ᑕᐃᑉᓯᒪᓂᒧᑦ ᒪᒃᑯᓚᐅᕐᓂᑦᑎᓐᓄᑦ, ᐃᓯᒪᑕᕐᔭᐊᖑᑎᓪᓗᑕ.
ᐆᒻᒪᑦ ᐃᓄᐃᓚᖅ ᐱᕈᐃᕗᖅ ᓯᒃᑭᒃᑕᖅᑐᓂᒃ.
ᐱᕕᒃᓴᖃᕐᓂᐅᓚᐅᖅᑐᑦ ᖃᒋᑕᐅᔪᑦ ᓯᓪᒐᓕᐊᑎᑐᑦ.

ᐃᓪᓚᖃᑎᒋᕙᖅ.

ᓄᖑᑦᑐᑦ ᓄᖑᑉᐳᑦ.
ᐊᒥᐊᒃᑰᔪᑦ ᐃᓱᖅᑲᖖᒋᑦᑑᒍᑦ
ᓄᖑᓯᐃᑦᑑᓪᓗᑎᒃ.

He brings me here when I am weak.
    We tumble like lovers.
Mirroring that rotten smile.   He takes me
    like Christmas past
to when we were young, puissant.
Fertile wastelands ripe with laughter.
Opportunities stamped out like cigarettes.

    I laugh with him.

What's gone is gone.
What's left   is forever
and eternal.

ᑲᑦᑐᕐᓂᖅ

ᐊᔪᓕᐅᖅᑲᔪᖅ ᐃᓅᓯᕋ
ᑕᓕᐅᒪᑎᑦᑎᕗᖅ ᐃᓱᒪᓕᐅᕈᓐᓇᕐᓂᕐᒥᒃ.
ᐊᕝᕕᐊᖅᑐᓕᐅᖅᐳᖅ ᓇᒧᓕᒫᖅ.
ᕐᑭᒡᒋᕆᐊᓕᑦ ᐊᑦᑐᖅᑕᓕᒫᒃᑲ.
ᐅᔭᒋᕆᐊᓕᒃᑲ ᐊᒥᓲᕗᑦ
ᓯᕗᓂᓐᓂ ᑭᖕᒍᓕᓐᓂ.

ᐃᓅᓯᖅ ᐊᒃᓱᕈᕐᓇᖖᒋᓐᓂᖅᓴᐅᕗᖅ
ᑕᕐᕋᐅᓗᓂ ᐅᖅᓱᖅ.
ᓇᕈᑐᐃᓐᓇᖅᐳᖕᒐ ᐃᒡᓕᓂᒃᑯᑦ ᐃᓄᐃᑦᓚᒥ.
ᓯᕕᑭᓈᕈᑎᑦ ᐱᕋᔭᖕᓄᑦ.
ᓇᕈᔮᑦ ᑎᑎᖅᑲᖕᒋᑦ ᐊᒻᒪᓗ ᐊᕙᓗᒧᑦ ᒥᖕᒍᐊᒐᖕᒋᑦ
ᑕᖅᓴᓕᐅᖅᓯᒪᕗᑦ ᓄᓇᓯᐅᑎᑯᑖᑦ ᐊᖅᑯᑎᖕᒋᓐᓂ
ᐅᕙᑦᑎᓐᓂᑦᓗ ᐊᖕᒋᕐᕋᐅᔅᓴᕗᑦ.

ᑕᓕᖅᐱᖕᒧᑦ ᓴᖕᒍᒋᑦ. ᓇᕈᔮᐅᕗᑦ ᒫᓂ.
ᓄᓇᓖᑦ ᐃᒥᐊᓗᒃᑖᕈᓐᓇᖅᑎᑦᑎᔪᑦ.
ᓂᕆᐅᒋᑦ ᐃᒻᒥᓂᒃ ᓴᐳᑎᔪᕆᐊᖅᑲᕈᕕᑦ.

ᐃᒐᕕᖕᒪ ᓂᐱᖕᒐ ᐋᖅᑭᒋᐊᕆᐊᖅᑲᖅᐳᖅ.
ᓇᑎᒃᑲᓗ ᓴᓃᓐᓇᖅᐸᒃᑲ.
ᐃᔾᔪᖅᓇᐃᑦᑐᖅᓯᐅᖅᑎᑐᑦ
ᑐᑭᓯᓇᓱᒃᑐᑐᑦ ᑐᖅᑯᒥᒃ.

ᓴᓂᖅ ᐊᒋᐊᖅᐳᖅ ᓇᑎᕋᕐᒥᒃ.
ᑏᓕᐅᕈᑎ ᐅᕕᖖᒋᐊᖅᐳᖅ.
ᐃᕐᖕᒍᓯᕋ ᐃᒻᒪᒃᐸᕋ.
ᐱᓱᒡᕕᒋᕙᒃᑕᒃᑲ ᓴᖅᑭᓯᒪᕗᑦ ᓇᑎᕐᒥ.
ᐃᒐᕕᖕᒥᑦ ᓵᒧᑦ.
ᓵᒥᑦ ᐃᑦᓗᕈᓯᓐᓄᑦ.
ᓂᐅᖅᑲᖅᐸᕋ ᑏᓕᐊᕋ ᐆᓇᓗᐊᕋᓗᐊᖅᑎᑦᓗᒍ
ᐊᒥᒐᕐᑯᖖᒋᓚᕋᓗ.

Inertia

My gridlock'd life
obscures reason.
Lays obstacles in every direction.
Hurdles at every step.
Detours pile
bumper to bumper.

Life is so much easier
as a greasy shadow.
Slip-sliding along the back trails.
The shortcuts of ne'er-do-wells.
Hobo glyphs and graffiti
mottle the railroad tracks
          and bring us home.

          Turn right.   Tramps here.   Town allows alcohol.
          Be ready to defend yourself.

My kitchen is out of tune.
My floors I sweep endlessly.
Like a monk
contemplating death.

Grit grinds over linoleum.
The kettle whistles.
My teacup fills.
Trails wear into the floor.
From kitchen to chair.
From chair to bed.
I sip the liquid too warm to bear
and hope it is enough.

ᐊᓂᓵᕆᕐ. ᓇᕈᕌᑦ ᑎᒍᔭᐅᓰᑦ ᑕᑯᔭᐅᔪᐊᕈᑎᒃ.

ᕿᑲᕈᓐᓇᙱᑦᑕᖓ ᓯᓂᒃᑐᖓ. ᓯᓐᓇᒃᑐᕐᓂᕐᓗᒃᐳᖓ.
ᕿᐱᒃ ᑎᒍᓗᒍ. ᒪᑉᐱᕐᓕ ᐃᒐᓛᖅ.
ᓈᓚᒍᒃ ᐅᓐᓄᐊᖅ.
ᓈᓚᒍᒃ ᐃᓪᓚᖅᑎᓪᓗᒍ, ᕿᐊᑎᓪᓗᒍ,
ᕿᐊᖀᓪᓚᒃᑕᖅᑐᖅ.
ᐆᒃᑐᕈᒃ ᒪᖑᑦᑎᔪᓐᓇᕐᓂᖓ.
ᐃᑉᐱᒋᒃᑭᑦ ᑲᑭᓂᖕᒋᑦ ᑮᓇᕐᓂ ᒥᖅᓱᖅᑕᖕᒋᑦ.

ᖃᐃᒋᑦ, ᒪᐅᖓ ᑐᐱᕆᕐ. ᐊᑦᑕᕐᓇᙱᑦᑐᖅ ᓛᓂ ᑐᐱᖅᕕᒃ.
ᐊᑭᖅᑲᙱᑦᑐᖅ.

ᐆ ᐸᓂᑉᓗᑉᕕᖅ!
ᒪᑐᔭᐅᓯᒪᓕᖅᓗᐊᕐᒪᑦ.
ᓱᓕ ᒪᑐᐃᖓᐃᓐᓇᖅᐳᖅ.
ᐃᓅᓕᕐᕕᐊᓂᓪᓘᓐᓃᑦ.

Get out fast.   *Tramps arrested on sight.*

I turn in my sleep.   Fitful.
Grab a blanket. Open a window.
Listen to the night.
Listen to Her laugh, cry,
moan.
Taste Her mischief.
Feel Her tattoo stitch across your face.

Come, camp here.   *Safe camp here.*   *No charge.*

O Sanatoria!
You may be closed.
Yet Her doors are always open.
Even on Christmas.

ᐃᑯᐊᓚᔪᒧᑦ ᑐᖁᑕᐅᓂᖅ

ᖁᐸᓄᐊᑦ ᐅᖃᓗᕋᐅᔭᖅᓂᖕᖓ ᓴᐃᒻᒪᖅᑎᑦᑎᙱᓚᖅ.
ᓯᕿᓂᖅ ᓂᐱᖕᒐᒍᖅ.
ᑕᖃᐃᖅᓯᖅᓇᙱᓚᖅ ᐃᖕᒋᐅᓕᒃᑐᒥ ᐳᒃᑕᑦᓗᓂ
ᐅᓐᓄᐊᒃᑯᑦ.

ᐅᕙᓐᓄᑦ ᐃᓯᔾᔪᒃᐳᖅ.

ᓴᐱᓕᖅᓂᖅ.
ᑕᒪᐅᖕᒑᓇᑐᐃᓐᓇᖅᓂᖅ.
ᐅᑕᖅᑭᐊᖑᑦᓗᓂ ᓄᖑᓴᖅᑕᐅᓂᖅ.
    ᐊᒃᓱᓂᖅ.

ᐅᕙᓐᓄᑦ ᐃᓯᔾᔪᒃᐳᖅ.

    ᐃᖅᑲᐅᒪᕕᑦ? ᑕᐃᑉᓯᒪᓂ
    ᐅᕙᑦᑎᓐᓂᒃ ᓇᒡᓕᒍᓱᒃᑎᑦᓗᒍ   ᐱᓐᓇᓱᑦᓗᓂᑎᒍᑦ.
    ᐃᖅᑲᐅᒪᕕᑦ?
    ᑲᑕᒃᑎᓚᐅᖅᑕᒍᑦ ᐃᒃᓯᕙᐅᑕᖅᔪᐊᖕᒋᓐᓂᑦ
        ᑕᐃᑲᙵᑦ
        ᐊᕙᓗᐊᓗᖕᒥᑦ.

ᐃᓯᔾᔪᒃᑕᖕᒋᑦ,
ᐃᑎᖅᑐᖅᓂᐅᒐᑦ ᐃᑯᐊᓚᔪᑦ,
ᓯᖁᐃᒐᖅᓗ ᐃᓯᒪᒥᒃ ᐆᒪᑎᒧᑦ.
ᑕᐃᒪᙵᓕᒫᖅ ᑕᐃᒪᐃᑉᐳᖅ.

Immolation

Birdsong offers no relief.
The sun doesn't shine.
There is no respite riding the waves
of the nighttime.

He whispers to me.

Resignation.
Futility.
Attrition.
        Lowliness.

He whispers to me.

Remember? Back when
he loved us   best.
Remember?
We threw their thrones
from
the
wall.

His whispers,
the sodomy of flames,
maligns the mind against the heart.
Time and time again.

ᐃᖅᑲᐅᒪᕕᑦ?
ᐃᓯᔾᔪᒍᓐᓇᓚᐅᖅᐳᒍᑦ ᐅᓂᒃᑳᖅᑐᐊᕐᒥᒃ ᐊᕐᓇᓗᑲᐅᑉ ᓯᐅᑎᖕᒐᓄᑦ
ᐊᓗᒃᑐᕐᓗᑕᓗ ᐃᑭᑦᑎᓐᓂᒃ
ᖃᐅᓇᓱᖕᓂᖕᒐᓂ.

ᐊᓂᒋᑦ, ᒥᖕᒎᑉ! ᐊᓂᒋᑦ, ᕿᒻᒥᕐᓘᑏ!
ᐅᑯᐊᒃ ᐊᒡᒑᒃ ᑲᐅᒃᑖᖅᓯᒪᔫᒃ ᓴᓗᒻᒪᓚᐅᖅᓯᒪᔾᔭᕈᓐᓃᖅᐴᑉ!
ᑕᕐᕋᖅ ᑐᑦᑐᖅ
ᓱᕈᐃᕗᖅ ᐱᓂᐊᕐᓂᖅᓯᒪᔭᒥᒃ. ᓯᐊᒻᒪᐃᕗᖅ ᑐᕐᑯᔪᓄᑦ ᐊᓯᐅᕕᖕᒥᒃ.
ᐃᒧᑦᓗᐃᕗᖅ ᖃᐅᒪᐅᑉ ᑕᓗᐊᓂᒃ.

ᓱᖕᒪᑦ ᒪᐅᖖᒐᐅᑎᕕᖖᒐ?
ᓱᖕᒪᑦ ᒪᓚᒃᐸᒃᐳᖕᒐ?

Remember?
We could whisper a tale into a maiden's ear
then lick our wounds
until dawn.

Out, spot! Out, cur!
These rough hands will ne'er be clean!
The shadow that falls
stains the vow.   Mars perdition.
Crimps the lampshade.

Why do you take me here?
Why do I go with you?

ᐅᑉᐱᕐᓂᖅ
Faith

“ᑖᓐᓇ ᐊᕐᓇᖅ ᑕᐅᑐᙵᕆᒪᓇᓚᐅᖅᐳᖅ, ᐅᔭᕋᐅᑲᒥ
ᑕᐅᑐᙵᔪᐊᕐᓂᕐᒥᓪᔫᓐᓃᑦ ᐱᔪᓐᓇᙵᕆᒪᓇᒃᑐᖅ.”
- ᒫᒡᒍᓇᑦ ᓗᐊᓇᓐᔅ

ᓴᓇᓯᒪᔪᖅ ᐃᔅᓯ

ᑯᑦᑎᑕᐅᓯᒪᔪᖅ ᐊᕐᓇᒍᑦ ᐅᑕᖅᑭᓂᕐᒥᒃ.
ᐃᔅᓴᒃᓯᒪᔪᖅ ᐊᕐᓇᓗᑲᒍᑦ
ᒥᙳᐊᕐᓂᕐᒥᒃ ᓴᓗᐊᕐᓇᖅᑐᓂᒡᓗ
ᒥᙳᐊᖅᓯᒍᖅ ᐅᒥᐊᑉ ᓯᒍᓂᐊᓂᒃ.
ᑯᑦᑐᓂ ᓇᑎᖕᒪᓄᑦ.
ᑖᒪᓂ ᕐᑯᓪᓗᕆᐊᑦ ᐱᕈᖅᐳᑦ
ᐅᐃᕚᑦ ᓇᓗᓇᐃᒃᑯᑕᖕᒪ ᐃᓵᕆᓐᓂᒃ ᒪᑐᐊᖅᓯᒪᒍᖅ.
ᑲᑎᑎᑕᐅᓂᕐᒧᑦ ᐊᑕᔪᖕᒪᑕ ᑲᓚᖕᒪ, ᒪᓚᓚᐅᖅᑐᖅ ᐱᔪᑐᕐᑲᕐᒥᒃ,
ᑲᓚᑉᐹ ᑐᓄᐊᓂ.

ᐅᖅᓱᕐᒧᑦ ᐸᔫᒐᖕᒪ
ᐸᔫᖅᐸᖕᒪ ᐃᔾᔪᕐᓇᐃᑦᑐᒧᑦ ᑎᐱᓕᐅᕈᑎᒥᑦ.
ᓯᐊᓖᖑᒐᖕᒪ ᐃᓯᒪᓂᕐᓄᑦ ᑐᒃᓯᐊᕐᓂᕐᓄᓪᓗ,
ᐅᔭᒥᐅᒐᖕᒪ ᓂᕗᖕᒪᔪᖅ ᓴᐃᒻᒪᖅᑎᑦᑎᓂᖕᒪᓂᑦ.
ᑖᓐᓇ ᐅᖅᓱᕐᒧᑦ ᐸᔪᖅ ᐃᔅᓴᒃᓯᒍᖅ
ᐊᓄᓇᕐᒧᑦ ᑎᒃᑯᐊᖅᑑᑎᓂᒃ.
ᐃᒥᕐᓗᒃᑐᖅ ᖃᐅᓯᕐᓂᒃ ᐊᖅᑯᑎᐅᑉ ᓵᑦᑐᔾᔭᖕᕆᓐᓂᒃ.
ᐊᖑᓯᓪᓗᓂ ᓯᓐᓇᒃᑐᕐᓂᕐᓗᖕᓂᒃ.
ᓂᐅᙳᒪᒃᑕᖅᐳᓪᓗ ᓱᓪᓗᓚᓄᑦ
ᐅᕙᓂᕈᕐᒧᑦ ᐃᑎᑎᕆᔪᒧᑦ.

ᑖᒃᑯᐊᓚᒫᑦ ᐊᓂᒍᖅᐸᓪᓚᐊᓃᑦ ᕐᑭᓪᓚᖅᐳᑦ
ᓱᕐᓗ ᓄᑎᖕᓂᐅᔮᖅᑐᑦ ᐊᓚᔫᔭᕐᒥ.

ᑎᓪᓚᒐᕐᓗᓂ ᐃᒃᐱᐊᕐᔪᖕᕆᓐᓂᒃ ᐅᕙᓂᕈᐃᑦ
ᒥᖅᓱᐊᐃᓐᓄᒡᓗᕆᓪᓗ ᐊᒻᒪᔪᖕᕆᑦ.
ᑭᖑᒧᖕᒫᖅ ᑭᓗᑦ ᐋᖅᑭᒃᓱᕐᓗᕆᑦ
ᐊᓚᒃᑐᑦᑎᐊᕐᓗᕆᑦ.

"She was doubly blind, not only stone
but unendowed with even a pretense of sight."
—Margaret Laurence

Artificial Extract

Our distilled Lady of Vigils.
        Our infused maiden
of Oils and Vinegars
        anoints the prow.
        Stains the wooded hull.
Where canker blossoms bloom
fleurs-de-sel over her eyes.
Her bridal train, a seasoned wake,
        trails in behind.

I am that greasy smoke
spilling from the holy censer.
        Vassal of Thoughts and Prayers,
        Pendant of His Swinging Benediction.
That oily fog rubbing itself
        along the weathervanes.
Carousing over wetted pavements.
Capturing rotten dreams.
To curlicue into culverts
        waistcoat   deep.

All these moments   glint
like   flaws in a gem.

To pick the pockets of shirtsleeves
and sweetly sew them shut.
To inverse unseemly stitches
madly torn out.

ᒥᖕᒍᐊᕈᑎᐅᒍᖅ ᓴᐅᓂᓐᓄᑦ ᐅᔭᕋᙳᖅᓯᒪᔪᓄᑦ.
ᐅᓗᒃᓴᖅᓇᖅ ᐃᒪᖅᒥ ᐃᖢᐊᖅᑕᐅᑎᒐ.
ᓱᕈᖅᐳᖅ ᐃᒪᖅᒥ.
ᐃᑲᔫᓯᐊᑦ ᐃᖢᐊᖅᓂᖅᒥᑦ.

ᐅᓇᓕ ᐱᓗᐊᓕᖅᑐᖅ.
ᐃᔅᓯᓕᐊᒍᑦ ᐃᓴᕋᖅᑐᐊᒃᑯᑦ.

Salve of my coral bones.
Poultice of my hydropathy.
Corrupts below the surface.
        The benefits of luxury.

This is getting out of hand.
Our tincture of contraband.

“ᓯᕗᓂᐅᑎᕐ, ᐅᕐᑲᖅᐸᖕᒐ, ᓯᕗᓂᐅᑎᑦ ᓱᕋᐃᒍᑦ ᐸᖅᑐᔪᖕᒋᓐᓂᒃ;
ᓂᕕᖕᒐᒍᓪᓗ ᓇᒧᑦ ᖃᐅᔨᒪᖖᒋᑕᓐᓄᑦ.”

—Hᐋᕐᑦ ᑯᕋᐃᓐ

ᐅᐸᕐᑯᓴᐅᓂᖅ

ᐅᐊᑦᑎᐊᕈᕐᓂᓴᖅ ᐃᓯᕕᑉᐸᓪᓕᐊᒍᖅ ᓯᒍᓂᓐᓄᑦ.
ᓯᒍᓂᒃᓴᖅ ᕿᒪᒃᐸᓪᓕᐊᕗᑦ.
ᓴᖅᑭᑦᑕᒐᐅᒍᑎᑦ ᖁᖖᒋᐊᒐᕐᒥ
    ᐃᓱᓕᑉᐸᓪᓕᐊᔪᒥᒃ.

ᓂᖅᑐᐃᕕᐅᑉ ᓯᕗᓂᐅᑎᖕᒋᑦ ᓂᐸᐃᑦᑑᓕᖅᐳᑦ.
ᓯᕗᓂᕐᓂᕙᓚᐅᖅᑕᖕᒋᑦ ᐅᓂᒃᑳᖅᐳᑦ ᐅᐊᑦᑎᐊᕈᕐᓂᓴᕐᒥᒃ
ᐱᓇᓱᑦᑎᐊᖅᑎᓪᓗᑕ ᓱᓕ.
ᒫᓐᓇᓕ, ᐃᓱᒪᒋᔪᒪᒧᓐᓃᖅᐸᒍᑦ
ᓂᖅᑐᐃᕕᖕᒥᒃ ᑲᒪᔩᑦ ᓯᕗᓂᐅᑎᖃᕕᖕᒧᑦ ᒪᔪᖅᑎᓪᓗᒋᑦ.
ᐃᖅᑲᖅᑐᐃᔭᑦ ᒥᙳᐊᖅᐳᑦ ᐅᖅᓱᕐᒥᒃ ᓯᕗᓂᐅᑦ ᓂᐱᖃᐅᑎᖕᒋᓐᓂᒃ
ᓂᕕᖕᒐᑖᖕᒋᓐᓂᓪᓗ.
ᐅᖃᓕᒫᖅᑎᑦ,
ᐊᖅᓵᖅᑕᐅᒍᑦ ᓯᕗᓂᐅᑦ ᐱᑐᖕᒋᓐᓂᒃ,
ᑲᑎᖅᓱᕐᓕᑦ ᐅᐸᖅᑐᑦ ᓴᐃᒪᓃᓐᓇᖕᒐᓄᑦ ᐊᕐᓇᑦᑕ.
    ᖀᒥᓇᖅᑐᖅ ᐊᕐᓇᒍᑦ ᓂᐱᓕᐅᕈᑎᑦ ᓂᐱᖕᒋᓐᓄᑦ.

ᐊᓯᕈᕐᓂᐊᖅᐸᑦ ᓴᖅᑭᑦᑕᒐᖅ ᓯᕗᓂᐅᑦ ᓯᕗᓕᖅᐸ.

ᒥᕐᖑᐃᖅᓯᕐᕕᕕᑦ ᐅᔭᕋᖕᒥᑕ ᐃᓕᐅᖅᑲᖅᓯᒪᓂᖕᒋᑦ ᐆᓪᓚᑎᐅᔫᖅᐳᑦ.
ᑖᓚᕈᖅᓯᒪᔪᑦ ᓇᐹᖅᑐᑦ ᓇᑲᑕᐅᓂᖕᒋᑦ
ᐆᑕᖅᓯᒪᔪᑦ ᖃᕐᔪᑦ ᓇᑉᐸᖅᓯᒪᒍᑦ.
ᕿᖅᓱᑕᖅᓯᒪᔪᖅ ᐅᔭᕋᖕᒥ
ᐅᔭᕋᐅᔭᖖᒍᖅᐳᖅ ᐊᕐᓇᑦᑕ ᓴᐃᒪᓂᖕᒐᓄᑦ.

"The bells, I say, the bells break down their tower;
And swing I know not where."
—Hart Crane

Summons

The past unfurls before you.
The future lies behind.
You are a slide in a show
playing out of time.

The temple bells no longer sound.
Their records knell days past
when we gave a damn.
Now, we cannot be bothered
with sextons to climb the belfries.
Prefects to oil the bows and cannons.
The deacons,
benched from their bell ropes,
gather the faithful solely by Her grace.
Our loathsome Lady of Cassette Tapes.

Please change the slide at the sound of the bell.

Your rock garden is heart shaped.
Tarred tree stumps
cauterize arrows in place.
A tourniquet of stone
mortars Her Worship's grace.

ᖄᓚᖅᓯᒪᔪᑦ ᐃᒐᐅᑉ ᑐᖅᑐᐊᖏᑦ
ᐃᔾᔪᖅᑎᖅᓯᒪᔪᑦ ᓂᐲᑦ ᑎᒍᔭᐅᒪᔪᑦ
ᐃᑯᐊᓚᔫᑉ ᓴᓂᐊᓂ ᐅᖃᓪᓚᖃᑎᒌᒃᑐᓄᑦ
ᐃᑎᔪᕐᒥᒃ ᐅᖃᐅᓯᓚᖕᓄᑦ, ᐃᔾᔪᕐᓇᐃᓗᐊᖅᑐᑦ, ᐃᑉᐱᖕᓇᓗᐊᖅᑐᑦ.
ᐅᕙᒍᓪᓗ
ᓴᕐᕙᐅᔾᔭᐃᒃᑯᑎᖃᖕᒋᓐᓇᖅᑕ
ᑲᑕᓚᕈᑦᑕᓗ ᐊᑯᖅᑕᐅᔾᔮᖕᒋᑦᑐᒍᑦ.

ᓴᖑᓂᖅ ᒪᓚᕐᑯᔭᐅᔪᓂᒃ ᑐᕐᑯᑕᐅᔾᔪᑕᐅᔪᓐᓇᖅᐳᖅ.
ᑭᓯᐊᓂᓚ ᒪᓂᒪᔪᖅᑲᓇᐊᖅᑲᖅᐳᖅ.

Caramelized stovepipes
deglaze voices held hostage
to firelit conversations
that strike too deep, too pure, too raw.
And we are
without a lifeline
nor the safety of a net.

To deviate courts execution.
But something's got to give.

“ᑭᓱᒥᑦᓗ ᐊᓐᓄᕌᙳᐊᖃᕐᓂᐊᖅᐸ ᑖᓐᓇ ᐊᕐᓇᑯᓗ
ᖃᐅᑉᐸᑦ ᖃᒡᒋᓕᖅᐸᑕ?”

—*The Velvet Underground*

ᐃᓄᙳᐊᑦ

Notre Dame des Blasphèmes
expire la fumée qui brûle les yeux.
Les sacrés parfums des cendriers
où nous flagellons nos familiers
en vénérant nos âmes coupables.
Nos esprits tremblant du tabernacle.

ᑯᒻᒧᓂᐅᓂᖅᑐᑦ ᐅᕐᕉᔭᕋᑦ ᐅᑦᑐᕆᐊᓂᒃ ᓴᓐᓂᖓᔪᙳᐊᓂᒃ.
ᒪᑦᓕᖅᑎᑦᑎᕋᑦᓗ ᐃᒪᕙᖕᒥᒃ ᐋᖓᑦᑐᒥᒃ.
ᓴᒡᓗᔪᒥᒃ ᑐᓂᓯᑦᓗᓂᒋᑦ, ᐅᖃᐅᓯᑦ
ᒥᐊᖅᑕᐅᕋᑦ ᐅᖃᖕᒋᓐᓂᑦ
ᐃᒪᐅᑦᓗ ᐃᑭᐊᓅᖅᐳᑦ.

ᐊᕐᓇᕋᑦ ᐱᓱᒍᓐᓇᙱᑦᑐᓄᑦ,
ᐊᓈᓇᕋᑦ ᖁᕝᕕᐅᕐᓂᕐᒧᑦ,
ᐃᓕᓴᕆᔭᐅᔪᒪᕋᖅ. ᑐᓂᕐᕈᓯᐊᕈᒪᕋᖅ.
ᓂᖅᑐᖅᑕᐅᔪᒪᕋᖅ.
ᒥᖑᐊᒐᖅ ᕿᔪᖕᒧᑦ, ᐃᒪᐃᔭᐃᔾᔪᑦ ᑯᑐᒡᕕᒃ,
ᐱᓂᕐᓗᒃᑕᐅᓂᖅ.

ᕿᒃᓵᒃᑐᒃᑯᑦ ᐃᑦᑎᙳᐊᒃᑯᑦ,
ᑕᓗᓂ ᑐᙳᔪᐊᖓᔪᓂᒃ,
ᑐᓂᕐᕈᓯᐅᑎ ᑐᓂᖅᑲᖅᑕᐅᕋᖅ ᐅᑉᐱᕐᓂᕐᒥᒃ ᑕᒻᒪᖅᓯᒪᔪᓄᑦ.
ᑭᓇᐅᓂᕐᒥᓂᒃ ᓇᓗᓇᐃᙱᑦᑐᖅ ᖃᕿᐊᓕᖅᑐᖅ ᓴᔪᐊᓪᓖᖅᐳᖅ
ᐊᒥᒐᖅᓯᒐᓗᐊᖅᑐᓂ ᒎᑎᒥᒃ.
ᐱᙳᔪᑦ ᐊᕐᓇᑦ ᓯᓚᐃᑦᑐᑦ
ᑲᑕᒃᑎᑕᐅᓯᒪᒐᑦ ᑕᑯᔭᐅᔪᓐᓇᕐᑯᑦᓗᒋᑦ ᐃᔾᔨᔪᓄᑦ
ᑐᓴᕈᒪᔪᓄᑦ
ᖃᐅᔨᔪᒪᑐᐃᓐᓇᖅᑐᓄᑦ.

"And what costume shall the poor girl wear
To all tomorrow's parties?"
—*The Velvet Underground*

Effigies

Notre Dame des Blasphèmes
expire la fumée qui brûle les yeux.
Les sacrés parfums des cendriers
où nous flagellons nos familiers
en vénérant nos âmes coupables.
Nos esprits tremblant du tabernacle.

The celebrants stagger the Southern Cross.
Writhe drunken seas.
Giving them the lie, the word
heaves from their mouths
to join the underneath.

Notre Dame des Lames,
Our Mother of Tears,
demands tribute. Sacrifice.
Homage.
Linseed oil, cheesecloth,
trauma.

In mournful mauves,
in veils of violet,
the plate passes between heretics.
The anonymous repentant twitching
to eke out God.
Strung out ingénues
brought low to suffer the prying eyes
of inquiring minds
who simply need to know.

ᒪᒥᐊᑦᑐᖅ ᐱᐅᙱᓐᓂᕐᒥᓂᒃ

ᐊᖏᕐᕋᖅᑲᙱᑦᑐᖅ ᓯᓂᖕᓂᖅ
ᐊᓯᙱᓚᖅ ᐊᐃᑉᐸᖅᑖᕆᒪᔪᓂᒃ.
    ᓯᒃᑭᒃᑕᖅᑐᖅ ᐃᑯᒪᕐᔪᐊᒥᑦ.
ᑎᑦᓚᒐᖅᐳᖅ ᐃᓱᒪᒃᑯᑦ ᐱᙵᐊᕐᓂᐅᙳᐊᖅᑐᓂ.

ᑭᑭᐊᖕᓂᒃ ᐃᑦᓚᓚᐊᖑᓯᒪᔪᒧᑦ
    ᕿᑭᕐᕌᖅᐳᒧᑦ ᐊᒃᑕᕈᓯᒃᑐᑕ.

    ᒪᓯᖕᒥ ᐃᕙᒃᓯᒐᑯᑖᒥ ᐃᖅᑲᓗᒐᑦ
    ᒥᒃᑭᒃᐳᑦ ᐊᑕᔪᖓᓂᒃ.
    ᐃᒻᒪᒃᑐᑦ ᒪᐅᓇᖏᑦ ᑳᐅᒐᓚᐊᖑᔮᖅᐳᑦ.

ᐊᕐᓇᕗᑦ ᐅᑉᐱᕐᓂᖏᓐᓄᑦ ᑐᕐᑯᑕᐅᓯᒪᔭᓄᑦ
ᐃᒻᒥᓂᒃ ᑐᓂᕐᕈᑎᕗᖅ
ᐊᕐᓇᓗᑲᑯᓗᖕᓄᑦ.
ᑮᓇᐅᔭᕐᒧᑦ £-ᒧᑦ.
    2p-ᕌᖅᐳᖅ ᐴᖅ ᐊᑕᐅᓯᖅ.

    ᐃᔾᔫᒃ ᖁᕝᕙᐅᕐᒧᑦᑑᑕᖅᐴᒃ
    ᐅᔭᕋᑐᑦ ᒪᒥᐊᓐᓂᕐᒧᑦ.
    ᓴᐸᖓᓚᒃ ᐊᓈᓇᕗᑦ
    ᒪᓚᖃᑎᑮᒃᑐᓄᑦ ᐊᕐᓇᓗᑲᕐᓄᑦ
    ᐊᓪᓚᖏᑕᓗ ᐃᓄᓚᙳᐊᖏᑕ ᐋᖅᑭᒃᓯᒪᓂᖏᑦ
        ᐃᑎᖅᑐᖅᑕᐅᔪᒪᓂᕐᒥᒃ ᐱᔪᒪᓂᐅᕗᑦ.

ᑳᐅᒐᓚᐊᖑᔮᖅᑐᑦ ᐃᒧᓯᕗᑦ ᑲᓗᖕᒥᒃ.
ᐊᒦᓚᖅᑐᑦ, ᐊᓚᒃᓯᒪᔪᑦ, ᐱᔪᒪᓂᕐᒧᑦ ᑕᑯᒥᓇᙱᑦᑐᑦ.
ᐊᖏᕐᕋᕐᒥ ᓴᓇᐅᒐᑦ ᐃᔾᔪᕐᓇᐃᑦᑐᑦ ᐅᑯᖓᕗᑦ ᓱᓪᓖᖑᑦᓗᑎᒃ,
    ᐊᑲᖅᓯᙱᑦᑐᑦ ᐊᓄᖏᓐᓂᒃ.

Penitent

Shelterless sleep
entertains no suitors.
        Smirks from hell.
Steals the guise of fantasy.

To bed nails
        we tread gently.

        Cattail minnows
        nibble Her slip.
        Barnacle knuckles pucker Her fingertips.

Our Lady of Martyrs
propositions Herself
by the petal.
By the pound.
        Tuppence a bag.

        Weeping eyes cauterize
        in stony contrition.
        Our Beaded Mother
        of virginal processions
        and finger positions
                courts sodomy.

Bar knuckles fold at the seam.
Chipped, cracked, willingly obscene.
Homespun saints bent cruelly,
        resentful of the bit.

ᐅᓂᖓᔭᒃᑎ

ᐃᓴᕈᖅᑕᖅ ᓂᐅᖓᔪᖅ. ᐊᑭᕈᓴᒃ ᐃᒃᓱᓇᖅᑐᖅ.
ᐅᓂᖓᔭᒃᑎᐅᕗᖅ ᐊᔪᕆᖅᓱᐃᔨ.
ᐊᐅᓪᓚᖅᐳᖅ ᑎᑭᒃᑲᒥ.
ᐊᒃᑐᖅᑕᐅᙱᑦᑐᖅ, ᖁᐊᖅᓵᖅᑎᑕᐅᕗᖅ.

ᐃᖅᑲᖅᑐᖅᑕᐅᓂᖅ ᐅᓪᓗᒥ ᑎᑭᑉᐳᖅ, ᓄᑲᑉᐱᐊᒃᑲ!
ᐃᖅᑲᖅᑐᖅᑕᐅᓂᖅ ᐅᓪᓗᒥ ᑎᑭᑉᐳᖅ!

ᓈᓚᑦᑎᐊᖅᑐᖅ, ᐱᓐᓇᕆᔭᐅᔪᒪᔪᖅ.
ᓇᓚᐅᑦᑖᖅᑎ ᐃᑦᑕᕐᓂᓴᕐᒥᑦ
ᐅᖃᒻᒥᑕᒃᐳᖅ ᐊᓄᕋᔮᖅᑐᒧᑦ.

ᒥᑭᑦᑑᒐᓗᐊᒥᒃ ᓈᒻᒪᒃᓴᖅᐳᖓ, ᐊᖑᑏ.
ᐊᑏ, ᐱᔪᓐᓇᕈᕕᑦ,
ᐅᓪᓗᑕᒫᑦ ᑐᖁᖃᑦᑕᕋᓗᐊᕈᒪ ᓈᒻᒪᒃᐳᖅ
ᕿᒪᒃᑕᐅᙱᓯᖓᕈᒪ ᐱᔪᒪᓂᓐᓄᕐ!

ᐱᐅᙱᑦᑐᖅ ᖁᕕᐊᑦᑕᒃᑎᒐ ᐃᙱᙱᓚᖅ ᓇᓚᐅᑦᑖᖅᑐᓂᒃ.
ᐱᐅᔭᕇᖅᑐᓂᒃ ᑲᒪᙱᓚᖅ, ᓱᓴᓂᖅᑕᙱᓐᓂᒃ ᐅᖃᙱᓚᖅ.
ᐊᐅᖕᒧᑦ ᖃᐅᔨᓴᖅᑎᕆᕙᒃᐳᖅ ᐅᖃᖓᓂᒃ
ᐋᖓᔮᓴᕌᖓᒥ.
ᑲᖑᒃᓴᐃᕗᖅ ᐹ, ᐹ, ᐹ-ᖅᑐᓂ.
ᑲᓱᒃᑐᖅᑕ ᐃᒥᖅᑕᑦᑎᓐᓂᒃ.
ᐃᒥᕆᕐᔦ.

ᐃᒋᑕᐅᓯᒪᔪᖅ ᑯᒻᒧᓂᐅᓂᖅ
ᐅᖃᑦᑕ ᐊᑖᓄᖅᐳᑦ
ᐸᓯᔭᒃᓴᐅᓂᕐᒥᓂᒃ ᐊᑲᖅᓴᙱᓐᓂᐅᕗᑦ
ᐊᐅᒃᓴᖅᑐᑦ ᖃᓂᑦᑎᓐᓂ!

Mendicant

Gnarled branch.   Knotted lush.
Beggar priest of man.
Departs upon arrival.
        Uninvolved, nonplussed.

        The reckoning has come today, my boys!
        The reckoning has come today!

Hyper-compliant, eager as-you-please.
Prophet of the old guard
mutters to the breeze.

        I do not require much, Señor.
        Por favor, *if you please,*
        I'd rather die every day
        than outlive my dreams!

My profane rapturist sings no sooths.
Gilds no lilies, posits no truths.
Blood whets his tongue
when he is in his cups.
Spitting between his fingers.
        Sláinte.
                Bottoms up.

        The forsaken sacrament
        underneath our tongues
        resents mea culpas
        o'errunning our mouths!

ᑯᒻᒧᓂᐅᓂᕗᑦ ᓴᕕᕋᔭᒃ
ᖃᒃᑭᓐᓇᖅᐳᖅ ᓲᕐᓇᖅᑐᓂᓗ.
ᖁᑦᑎᒃᑎᑦᓯᕗᖅ ᑐᑭᓯᐅᒪᙱᑦᑐᓂᒃ.
ᐅᓂᖓᔭᒃᐳᖅ, ᐱᕐᓕᓕᖅᐳᖅ,
ᑐᖁᕗᖅ ᐊᖏᕐᕋᖅᑲᕋᓂ!

ᓂᖅᑐᒐᕋ ᑲᑕᒃᓯᒪᔪᖅ,
ᑲᙳᓯᙱᓚᖅ ᐅᖅᑲᓇᐊᖓ, ᓱᕋᐃᙱᑦᑐᖅ.
ᐅᖅᑲᐅᓯᖅᑲᖅᐳᖅ ᓂᙵᕐᓇᓇᔭᐅᔪᓂᒃ.
ᐅᕙᓐᓂᒃ ᐃᓕᑎᑦᑎᓚᐅᖅᐳᖅ
ᐃᓅᖅᑲᑎᒌᑦᑎᐊᖅᓂᖅ ᓇᓕᒧᒌᒍᓐᓃᖅᑐᖅ
ᐱᐅᒃᓴᖅᐳᖅ ᓄᑎᒃᓯᒪᔪᓂᒃ.

ᖁᕕᐊᓲᑎᖅᑲᓇᑦ ᐃᓅᑉ ᑲᑕᖕᓂᖓᓂᒃ, ᕿᑐᖅᖔᒃ.
ᐊᓕᐊᓇᐃᒍᓱᒋᑦ ᐱᓗᐊᓕᖅᓂᖅᒥᒃ.
ᐱᐅᙱᑦᑐᓕᓂᖅ ᐃᓱᒪᓂᑐᐃᓐᓇᐅᕗᖅ
ᐊᒻᒪᓗ ᐱᐅᙱᑦᑐᓕᔪᓐᓇᙱᓚᒍᑦ!

Our iron host
tastes bittersweet.
Exalts the insular.
Begs, starves,
DIES IN THE STREET!

My fallen idol,
minced no words, broke none.
Tongued the sore   points.
Taught me
that harmony   out of balance
favours disjoint.

Delight in the fall of man, child.
Take pleasure in excess.
For sin is but imagined
and we cannot transgress!

ᐅᔭᕋᒃ ᓇᐸᔪᖅ

Stone

I

ᐊᑖᓂ ᐆᒪ ᓄᓇᖅᑲᑎᒌᓪᓯᐊᑉ
ᐱᑦᑎᐊᕐᓂᖅ ᑲᑕᒐᖅᐳᖅ.
ᐅᖅᑲᐅᔭᑦ ᒪᖕᒋᖅᑐᓇᕗᑦ,
ᐅᖅᑯᒃᐸᓪᓚᐊᕗᑦ ᖅᑯᓚᓈᖕᓂᖕᒋᑦ,
ᓇᒡᒍᐊᒃᑲᓗ ᐅᑎᓚᖅᐳᑦ ᐃᔾᔪᕐᒧᑦ, ᐊᓐᓄᕌᒃᑲᓗ ᓄᓇᕋᕐᓄᑦ ᐱᕈᕐᕕᐅᓚᖅᐳᑦ.

ᑕᕐᓂᑦ ᐊᕙᓗᓯᕗᑦ ᐃᓗᕕᓐᓂᒃ.
ᐃᑎᒪᖕᒧᑦ ᐃᑎᒪᖕᒥᑦ, ᑐᒃᓯᐊᖅᐸᒃᐳᑦ ᓯᓚᒧᑦ.
ᐅᕙᓐᓂᑦ ᒪᑭᑎᑦᑎᓇᓱᒃᑐᑦ,
ᑭᓯᐊᓂᓚ ᑕᕐᕋᕋ ᐅᔭᕋᖕᒍᖅᐳᖅ
ᐊᑖᓂ ᐆᒪ ᓄᓇᖅᑲᑎᒌᓪᓯᐊᑉ.

ᑐᖅᑯᕋᐃᓂᖅᓯᐊᖅ ᑐᖅᑯᑦᑎᔪᓐᓇᖕᒋᓚᖅ ᐱᐅᖕᒋᓐᓂᕐᒥᒃ.
ᑐᖅᑯᑦᑎᔪᒪᒍᕕᑦ ᐊᑭᕋᕐᓂᒃ
ᐱᔪᒪᔭᖕᒋᓐᓂᒃ ᑐᓂᐅᖅᑲᕈᒃ.
ᐅᖅᑯᒪᐃᑉᐳᖅ ᐆᒻᒪᑎ ᐱᓯᒪᔪᖅ ᐱᔪᒪᔭᓚᒫᖕᒋᓐᓂᒃ.
ᓇᕐᑭᑕᐅᓂᕐᒧᑦ ᐅᖅᑯᒪᐃᑦᑐᐊᓗᖕᒧᑦ,
ᓇᐹᖅᑐᖅ ᓂᐅᖕᒐᒃᑐᖅ ᓇᑲᑉᐳᖅ.
ᓯᐅᕋᖅ ᐃᑦᑐᖕᒍᐊᓚᐊᖕᒍᔪᑦ ᓄᖕᒍᓴᖅᐳᑦ,
ᓯᓪᔭᖅᓯᕐᓂᕐᒧᑦ ᓯᕐᑯᑦᑎᓚᖅᐳᖅ.
ᐆᒻᒪᑎᒧᑦ ᐊᔪᐊᓚᕐᓇᖅᑐᖅ, ᑕᕐᓂᖕᒐ
ᐆᒪ ᓄᓇᖅᑲᑎᒌᓪᓯᐊᑉ.

I

Beneath this great city
decency falls away.
Leaves rust,
compost layer upon layer,
turning my joints to nutrients, my clothes flower beds.

Spirits circle my grave.
Palm to palm, they petition the sky.
Calling me to rise,
yet my shadow petrifies
beneath this stinking city.

Annihilation does not kill evil.
To destroy your enemy
simply grant their wishes true.
Heavy is the heart that has all it desires.
Burdened by its great weight,
a slouched tree breaks.
Sandcastles waste,
          dissolve beneath the waves.
To canker the heart,   the soul
          of this great city.

II

ᐃᔾᔪᖅ ᓱᕐᓗᓂᒃ ᓯᒥᒃᓯᕗᖅ.
ᐅᕐᑯᒃᓱᖕᓂᖅ ᓄᓇᒥᑦ ᖃᓗᕋᖅᑕᐅᔪᖅ
ᑎᐹᕐᑭᕗᖅ ᐅᕙᓂ ᓄᓇᖅᑲᑎᒌᕐᔪᐊᓂ.
    ᐅᕙᓐᓂᑦ ᐃᖅᑲᐅᒪᕗᖅ.
ᑕᐅᓇᓂ,   ᑕᐅᓇᓂᑐᕐᑳᓗᒃ,
ᓯᓂᒃᑐᖕᖓ ᕿᕐᑲᕈᓐᓇᙱᑦᓚᖕᖓ,   ᓯᓐᓇᒃᑑᒪᕗᖕᖓ.
    ᐃᓄᒃᐸᒃ ᓯᓂᒃᑐᖅ
ᓯᓐᓇᒃᑐᕐᓂᕐᓗᖕᒍᑦ ᐸᕝᕕᒋᔭᐅᔪᖅ ᓄᓇᒥᓪᓗ ᑐᑭᓕᐊᖅᑐᓄᑦ
ᓯᕐᑯᒥᑦᑐᓄᑦ ᕿᓪᓕᖅᑐᓄᓪᓗ ᑕᕐᓂᕐᔪᐊᒥᑦ.
ᐊᕙᓚᖕᖓᔪᖅ ᕐᑯᓚᐅᑦᑐᖅ
ᐊᑲᖅᓭᐅᑕᐅᙱᑦᓚᖅ
ᐆᒪᑎᒪ ᑰᖓᕐᓂᖕᖓᓄᑦ.
ᑖᓐᓇᓗ ᐃᒪᖕᖓ ᓱᕈᖅᓯᒪᕗᖅ   ᓂᖕᖓᐅᒪᔪᖅ
ᐊᑖᓂ ᐆᒪ ᓄᓇᖅᑲᑎᒌᔅᔪᐊᑉ.

II

Soil clogs my nostrils.
The stench of ozone and turned earth
permeates this hateful city.
          It remembers me.
Down,   deep down below,
I turn in my sleep,   fitful.
          A slumbering Giant
plagued by night terrors and ley lines
that crack and glisten the divine.
The branch that passes above
reconciles not
The spring of my heart.
This well of rot   seething
beneath this great city.

III

ᖁᐱᕐᕈᐊᕐᔪᐊᓗᐃᑦ
ᐅᐃᒻᒪᐃᕗᑦ ᐃᓱᒪᓐᓂᒃ
ᐅᖃᓪᓚᒃᑐᑦ ᐊᔪᓕᕐᓇᖅᑐᓂᒃ ᑭᓇᑐᐃᓐᓇᕐᒧᑦ.
ᐃᓯᔾᔪᒃᐳᑦ ᐃᔨᑫᖅᑐᐊᖑᔪᓂᒃ,
ᐅᖁᒻᒥᖅᓯᔭᑬᖕᒐᒥᒃ ᐃᖅᑲᐅᒪᓂᕐᒥᒃ.
ᒪᒪᑕᒃᐳᑦ ᕿᓄᐃᓵᕐᓂᖕᓂᒃ.
ᑕᒪᓐᓇ ᖁᕕᐊᑦᑕᖕᓂᐅᕙ,
ᓄᖑᓴᐃᔪᖅ ᑐᑭᓯᐅᒪᙱᓐᓂᖅ?

ᒎᑎᒥᒃ ᐊᑭᕋᖅᑐᕐᓂᑦ
ᓴᖅᑭᑎᑕᐅᓯᒪᙱᑦᑐᑦ ᓯᓚᕐᔪᐊᒧᑦ
ᓇᔪᖅᐸᒃᑲ ᐃᓂᖕᓂ.
ᐊᑭᕋᖅᑐᕐᓃᑦ ᑐᑭᓯᐅᒪᔭᐅᙱᑦᑐᑦ ᐃᓄᖕᓄᑦ ᒎᑎᒧᑦᓗ.
ᐃᓅᖅᑲᑎᒋᕙᒃᑕᒃᑲ ᐱᐅᙱᑦᑐᑦ.
ᑐᖁᓂᕐᒥᒃ ᑲᑉᐱᐊᓱᙱᑦᑐᑦ ᑖᒃᑯᐊ.
ᑖᖅᑐᒥ ᑕᑯᑎᑕᐅᓂᖃᙱᑦᑐᑦ.
ᐃᓱᖃᙱᑦᑐᒧᑦ.
ᕿᓐᓂᖅᑐᑐᐃᓐᓇᖅ ᐃᔾᔪᖅ. ᑐᐊᐸᒃ.
ᐊᕿᑦᑐᖕᒐᓂᖅ.
ᑖᓐᓇ ᐅᓗᓄᐊᓇᖅᑐᐊᓗᒃ ᐅᓚᒃ ᐱᖕᒋᓯᒻᒥᒃᓯᓇᓱᙱᑦᑎᐊᖅᐳᖅ.
ᐱᐅᒋᓛᖅᑲᙱᑦᑐᖅ.
ᐊᐅᓚᔾᔭᐃᔪᖅ ᐱᐅᙱᓐᓂᕐᒥᒃ.
ᐃᒻᒥᓂᒃ ᐃᒋᑦᑕᕐᓂᖅ ᐱᔪᒪᙱᑕᕋ.
ᖀᒥᖕᓂᐊᓗᒃ ᑭᒃᑯᓕᒫᕐᓂᒃ; ᑲᑎᖕᒐᑎᑦᑎᔪᖅ.
ᓄᓯᒃᓯᑦᓗᓂ ᖁᓛᓂᑦ ᐊᒻᒧᑦ
ᐊᑖᓄᑦ ᐆᒪ ᓄᓇᖅᑲᑎᒌᓪᔪᐊᑉ..

III

A million insects
swarm my thoughts
in tongues no one need endure.
They tell me secrets,
between mouthfuls of memory.
        Savouring my last nerves.
Is this bliss,
this devouring ignorance?

Blasphemies
ne'er intended for creation
share my bedrock.
Atrocities beyond man or God.
        The company I keep.
The grave is lost on their ilk.
No sunless revelation.
No ever after.
Just black dirt.   Gravel.
Stupidity.
This sinister veil pulls no punches.
Plays no favourites.
Excites perverse.
        The flailing about I can do without.
The indiscriminate hate;   to debase.
To pull above   below
        beneath this wretched city.

IV

ᓱᓂᕐᑎᐊᖕᒋᓚᖓ,
ᐱᔪᓐᓇᕐᓂᖃ ᐃᓱᒪᔪᓐᓇᕐᓂᕐᒥᒃ ᐃᖅᑲᐅᒪᔪᓐᓇᕐᓂᒥᒡᓗ
ᕿᒪᐃᓱᒪᕗᑦ ᐅᕙᓐᓂᒃ. ᕿᒫᕗᑦ ᐳᕙᓐᓂᒃ.
ᑲᔾᔮᖅᐳᖅ ᓈᒻᒪᒃᓯᓂᕐᒥᒃ
ᐃᓅᕐᑲᑎᖏᓐᓄᑦ ᑕᑯᔭᐅᓗᓂ.
ᐊᓯᖏᓐᓄᑦ ᐊᑭᓕᐅᑕᐅᓗᓂ.
ᐃᓕᓴᕆᔭᐅᓂᖅ ᒥᑭᓗᐊᖅᐳᖅ.
        ᐊᓯᕗᑦ ᑲᑕᒃᑎᑕᐅᒋᐊᖃᖅᐳᑦ.
ᐅᕙᑦᑐᑦ.   ᐃᓕᒃᑑᓂᐊᖅᑐᖅᑕᐅᖅ.
ᒪᑭᒋᐊᕐᓂᕐᑲᖕᒋᓚᖅ.
ᐱᐅᓕᔭᐅᓂᕐᑲᖕᒋᓚᖅ
ᐊᑖᓂ ᐆᒪ ᐃᒻᒥᓂᒃ ᓱᕐᓂᓂᐅᑉ.

ᓇᒡᓕᖕᓂᖅ ᐱᒋᐊᕈᓐᓇᖕᒋᓚᖅ   ᓱᓕᓂᕐᒥᑦ
ᑲᑕᒃᑎᑕᐅᓚᐅᖅᑳᖅᑎᓐᓇᑕ.
ᐊᓂᖅᓵᕈᓐᓇᐃᓪᓕᑎᑕᐅᕕᑕ
ᑕᕐᓂᒃᑯᑦ.
ᐃᑉᐱᒍᓱᒍᓐᓇᕐᓂᐅᑉ ᐃᑎᓂᖓ
ᐊᓕᒃᑐᖅᑕᐅᕗᖅ, ᑐᕐᑯᓕᑎᑕᐅᓪᓗᓂ ᓇᓗᓕᐅᖅᑲᓕᖅᑎᑕᐅᓪᓗᓂ.
ᐃᒪᕕᖕᒥ ᐊᓄᓇᕐᑲᖕᒋᑦᑐᒥ.
        “ᕿᓐᓂᖅᑕᒧᑦ ᖃᓂᕐᒧᑦ ᐅᔭᖅᑭᓯᒪᔪᒧᑦ”
ᓴᔪᓪᓛᖅᐳᖓ ᐅᐃᔾᔮᖅᐳᖓ ᑕᐅᓇᓂ ᐃᑎᔪᕐᒥ.
ᕐᑯᓕᓐᓂ, ᓱᓐᓇᒃᑐᖅᑐᑦ ᐃᖅᑯᒻᒪᖅᐸᓪᓕᐊᓕᖅᐳᑦ,
        ᐊᓕᒃᓯᒪᔪᖅ ᑮᓇᖅ ᐃᓱᒪᒥᑦ ᐊᓯᐅᓕᖅᐳᖅ.
ᕿᒻᒥᑦ ᖁᓪᓗᒃᑕᖅᐳᑦ ᓱᓂᒃᑐᑎᒃ
ᕿᑦᑐᒃᑎᑦ ᐹᕐᖓᖓᕗᑦ
        ᐱᓐᓇᔮᖅᑐᑦ.
ᑖᓐᓇ ᒥᑭᑦᑐᖅ ᖁᐊᖅᓵᕐᓇᖅᑐᖅ,
        ᑖᓐᓇ ᑕᑯᑎᑕᐅᓂᖅ,
ᓈᒻᒪᒋᕙᐃᑦ
ᐊᑖᓂ ᐆᒪ ᓄᓇᖅᑲᑎᒌᒡᔪᐊᑉ.

IV

Sleeping rough,
the acumen of thought and memory
evades me. Escapes me.
Craves fulfilment
in the eyes of others.
At the expense of others.
Validation is not enough.
Others should fall.
As I have. As you will.
There is no revival.
No redemption
beneath this self-pity.

Love cannot begin true
until one has fallen out of.
Have had the wind knocked out of
one's soul.
One's emotional breadth
violently torn, left withered and listless.
In windless oceans.
"With black lips baked"
I twitch and turn leagues below.
Above, dreamers start awake,
A torn visage fading out of mind.
Dogs wince in their sleep
while cats settle Sphinxlike
in satisfaction.
This inch of terror,
this revelation,
pleases them
beneath this ancient city.

V

ᑭᓈᓗᖕᒐ ᐃᓄᐃᑦ.
        ᖃᓄᑭᐊᖅ ᐃᒃᑯᐊ ᓴᐅᓯᕗᒃᐸᑦ ᐊᖖᒋᐊᖕᒋᓐᓂᒃ
ᐆᒻᒪᑎᒪ ᐊᐅᖅᑲᐅᑎᖕᒋᓐᓂ.
ᐲᔭᐃᔪᖅ ᑕᖅᑲᒪ ᖁᕋᑦᑕᖕᓂᖕᒐᓂᒃ.
ᑐᖁᓴᐅᑎᖕᒋᑦ   ᑲᒪᓇᖅᑐᑦ
        ᐃᓄᐊᖅᓯᓯᒪᖕᒪᑕ ᓄᓇᕐᔪᐊᒥᒃ.
ᑐᐊᕖᓐᓇᖅ ᐱᓇᓱᒃᑕᒧᑦ,
ᐃᔅᓴᐃᕗᑦ ᐃᒪᖅᑲᐅᑎᒥᒃ,   ᓱᕈᐃᕗᑦ ᓄᓇᒥᒃ
ᑕᐅᑐᖕᓂᑦᑎᓐᓂᒃ ᖀᒥᖕᒪᑕ.
ᖃᑭᒍᓛᖅᐸᖕᒐ   ᑕᕝᕗᖖᒐᑦ ᑕᓯᕐᔪᐊᕐᒥᑦ
ᐲᕐᓗᖕᒐᓗ ᐃᖁᒻᒥᔭᐅᓂᕐᒥᒃ
        ᐋᓐᓂᐊᓕᖕᒥᑦ ᐃᒪᕐᒥᒃ.
ᓴᐃᒪᖅᑎᑦᑎᓗᖕᒐᓗ   ᓱᑲᖕᒐᔪᒧᑦ ᖃᓂᕐᒧᑦ
ᐊᑦᑕᕈᓱᒃᐸᖅ ᐱᓂᐅᓯᓂᖅ.
ᑲᑎᖅᓱᒐᖅ ᓴᖅᑭᑉᐸᖅ.
ᑲᑕᒐᖅᐸᕐᓗ ᐊᑯᓂ ᐊᒻᒧᑦ,
ᑑᕐᖕᒐᑦ ᐃᓪᓗᖕᒋᑕ ᐊᑖᓂ ᓯᕐᓗᐊᕐᓄᑦ.
ᓄᖅᑲᖅᑎᑦᑎᔭᖅᑐᖅᑐᑦ ᐋᓐᓂᑕᐅᓂᕐᒥᒃ,
ᖀᒥᖕᓂᕐᒥᒃ,   ᐋᓐᓂᖅᓯᒪᓂᕐᒥᒃ

        ᑕᕝᕗᓂ ᓄᓇᖅᑲᑎᕇᕐᔪᐊᕐᒥ.

V

The effluvia of man.
How they do bury their secrets
in the ventricles of my heart.
Mining the coral of my veins.
Their poisons legion
that they may murder the world.
Hell bent for leather,
they tinct the well, spoil the land
to spite our eyes.
That I may rise ‘neath this Great Slave
to release the embrace
of diseased waves.
And bless with pursed lips
tender deliverance.
The compact manifest.
To descend at length below,
in the cellar with the ghosts.
To end the hurt,
the hate, the pain

of this great city.

ᐃᑯᐊᓚᔪᖅ

Fire

ᓇᐹᖅᑐᓄᑦ

ᐃᒡᓗᑐᕐᑲᖅᑐᑦ ᐅᕙᖅᑐᔪᑦ ᐊᓄᓂᒥ,
ᐅᓇ ᓇᐹᖅᑐᕐᑲᕐᕕᒃ ᓂᓪᓕᐊᒍᖅ.
ᐃᓴᕐᕈᑕᖅ ᖃᓂᑦᑐᖅ ᓇᑲᐤᕈᓕᑦᑎᒍᖅ.
ᖃᓂᓐᓂᖅᓴᒻᒪᕆᖕᒥᑦ, ᐃᑯᒪ.
ᐊᑖᑕᑦᓯᐊᑦ ᐅᕐᕈᒍᑦ, ᐊᔭᒃᑕᐅᔦᑦ ᐃᓂᖕᒋᓐᓂᑦ.
        ᐊᑕᐅᓯᐊᒃᑲᓐᓂᖅ, ᐅᕐᑲᖅᐳᖅ.
        ᐊᑕᐅᓯᐊᒃᑲᓐᓂᖅ ᖁᔭᓈᖅᑕᐅᓗᑐᓂ, ᐅᕐᑲᖅᐳᖅ.
        ᐊᑕᐅᓯᐊᒃᑲᓐᓂᖅ ᐊᖕᒋᖅᑕᐅᖖᒋᓪᓗᑐᓂ, ᐅᕐᑲᖅᐳᖅ.
        ᖃᓄᒃᑲᓐᓂᕐᓕ ᐱᓂᕐᓗᒃᑲᔭᕐᒪᑕ?
        ᐅᓖᑦᑎᓐᓂᒃ ᑐᕐᑯᑦᑎᒃᑲᓐᓂᕐᓗᑎᒃ? ᐅᕐᑲᖅᐳᖅ.

ᐊᓈᓇᑐᕐᑲᖅ ᑮᓯᒍᖅ ᑯᓪᓗᖕᒐᓂᒃ.
ᐅᓇ ᐊᔭᐅᒃᐱᐊᖅ, ᐅᓇ ᐊᔭᐅᒃᐱᐊᖅ, ᐅᕐᑲᖅᐳᖅ.
ᖃᐃᔪᑦ ᓄᓇᒥ ᓴᓂᐅᑎᒐ, ᐅᕐᑲᖅᐳᖅ.
ᖃᓗᕋᐅᑎᖖᒐ ᐅᐃᒃᓴᓐᓂᒃ, ᐅᕐᑲᖅᐳᖅ.
ᐱᐅᓂᖅᓴᒻᒪᕆᒃ, ᓄᓕᐊᖅᑖᕈᑎᒍᕕᖖᒐ. ᓵᓚᐅᔭᖖᒋᑦᑐᒥᒃ.
ᕿᐊᖕᒋᓪᓗᑎᓪᓕ, ᐅᕐᑲᖅᐳᖅ.
        ᑕᒪᑐᒥᖕᒐ ᑕᑯᔦᒪᓇᔭᖅᑐᑦ, ᐅᕐᑲᖅᐳᖅ.
        ᑕᑯᔦᒪᑐᐃᓐᓇᕋᔭᖅᑐᑦ.

ᐋᓪᓚᑕᕐᑲᖖᒋᓚᖅ ᐃᓃᖅᓯᒐᔭᖅᑐᓂᒃ.
ᓄᓇᓕᖕᓂ ᐱᑦᑎᐊᖖᒋᓐᓂᕐᒥᒃ.
ᐅᕐᑲᐅᔾᔪᓐᓇᕋᓗᐊᖅᐳᑎᑦ ᑭᓯᐊᓂ ᑐᓵᔦᒪᖖᒋᓚᑎᑦ.
ᓯᒍᓂᐊᒍᑦ, ᑐᑭᓯᐅᒪᑦᑎᐊᖅᑐᓄᑦ ᐊᖕᒋᕈᑎᓂᒃ ᐱᓚᐅᖖᒋᓐᓂᕐᓂ
ᐅᕝᕙᓗ ᐱᓂᐊᕐᓂᕋᖅᑕᓂᒃ.
ᐊᑭᓖᓚᐅᖅᐳᑎᑦ ᐱᔦᓐᓇᐅᑎᓂᒃ
ᐅᓐᓄᐊᒃᑯᑦ
ᐃᑯᐊᓪᓚᐃᓚᐅᖅᐳᕐᓗ ᐃᒡᓗᑐᕐᑲᕈᓗᖕᒥᒃ.

ᖁᕕᐊᓱᒃᑐᒃᓴᐅᒍᑎᑦ, ᐅᕐᑲᖅᐳᖅ.
ᐃᕝᕕᕈᓗᒃ ᐃᒻᒥᓂᒃ ᐅᐱᕆᔦᒃᓴᐅᒍᑎᑦ.

ᐃᖅᑲᐅᒪᒋᑦ ᑭᓇ ᐃᑯᒪᒥᒃ ᐃᑭᑦᑎᓚᐅᕐᒪᖖᒌᑦ, ᐅᕐᑲᖅᐳᖅ.
ᐃᖅᑲᐅᒪᒋᑦ ᑭᓇ ᐃᑯᒪᒥᒃ ᐃᑭᑦᑎᓚᐅᕐᒪᖖᒌᑦ.

For The Trees

Like an old house leaning into the wind,
this forest groans.
A branch snaps nearby.
Closer still, a match.
Grandfathers fall, uprooted.
        Once more, he says.
        Once more renounced, he says.
        Once more denied, he says.
        What's the worst they could do?
        Kill us again? he says.

Old Mother bites her thumb.
A crutch, a crutch, she says.
Hand me my rake, she says.
Go dig me a new husband, she says.
Better yet, a wife. A fighter.
Just don't cry, she says.
        They'd love to see that, she says.
        They just would.

No strangers to overtaking.
To civil disobeying.
You dish it out but can't take it.
Without prior, informed consent
or commitment.
You put paid to rights
in the middle of the night
and lit an old house on fire.

I hope you're happy, she says.
I hope you're fucking proud.

Remember who struck this match, she says.
Remember who struck this match.

ᓄᓇᒥᒃ ᐊᖅᓵᖅᓯᓂᖅ

ᓇᐹᖅᑐᖅᑲᖅᕕᒃ ᓂᐱᑭᑦᑐᒥᒃ ᓂᓪᓚᐊᕗᖅ
ᐅᒥᐊᖅᔪᐊᖅᑐᑦ ᒪᓪᓕᖅᑐᒥ.
ᖁᔪᖕᒋᑦ ᖁᐊᕗᑦ, ᓱᕋᖖᒋᒃᑲᓗᐊᖅᑐᑎᒃ.
ᐃᓱᒪᒋᑦ, ᐅᐊᑲᓐᓚᖕᒎᒃ ᐃᒃᑯᐊ ᖁᔪᑦ
ᐊᑭᒋᐊᖅᑐᑦ.

ᐃᒻᒥᓂᒃ ᐱᐅᒋᔪᑦ. ᖃᐅᔨᒪᖖᒋᑖᑦ?
ᐃᓚᖁᓱᖅᑲᑦᑕᖖᒋᓪᒪᑕ
ᐃᓚᖁᒋᔭᖃᐊᖅᑲᖅᑕᖕᒋᓐᓂᒃ?
ᑎᒍᔭᐅᕈᓗᒡᓚᑦ.
ᐊᑦᑐᕐᒋᖅᑕᐅᓚᑦ ᐅᒥᐊᖅᔪᐊᑉ ᓯᕗᓂᐊᓄᑦ, ᐊᐳᖅᑕᖅᓚᑦ
ᒪᓪᓚᖅᓂᕐᒐᓄᑦ ᐃᓅᓯᐅᑉ ᓄᑖᑉ
ᐃᐱᑲᓴᒡᓗᑎᒃ.
ᐃᓚᑎᓐᓂᐊᖅᑕᕗᑦ ᐅᑯᐊ ᓴᔪᕐᓂᖅᒥᒃ.

ᖁᑳᒃᑐᒥᒃ ᑕᖅᓴᖅᑲᖅᐳᑦ ᓇᐹᖅᑑᑉ ᐅᖅᑲᐅᔭᕐᒋᑦ ᐅᓇᑕᖅᑐᒃᓴᑦ
ᐊᐅᒃᑕᔪᓂᒃ ᐊᒃᑐᕐᒋᐅᑎᔭᖅᐳᑦ ᐅᑕᖅᑭᕗᓪᓗ.
ᐊᓐᓅᖅᑦᑎᐊᖅᓯᒪᔪᑦ ᐅᓇᑕᖅᑎᒃᓴᑦ ᑲᓇᑕᒧᑦ ᖁᕐᓕᓯᖅᓂᒃ
ᑐᒥᔭᖅᑐᖅᑐᑦ.

ᑕᒪᓐᓇ ᓴᖖᒋᓂᐊᓗᒃᑎᓐᓂᒃ ᓴᖅᑮᔭᖅᑎᑦᑎᓂ ᓇᓗᓇᐃᖅᓯᖖᒋᓪᒫᑦ
ᖃᓄᑎᒋ ᓇᒡᓚᒋᖕᒪᖕᒎᒃᑭᑦ?
ᖃᓄᑎᒋ ᓱᑲᓐᓇᖅᑐᖅ ᓴᖕᒋᓂᖅᑲᓇᐊᖅᑲᖅᐸ ᖃᐅᔨᑎᓐᓂᐊᕋᑭᑦ
ᖃᓄᑎᒋ ᐸᖅᑭᔪᒪᖕᒪᖕᒎᒃᑭᑦ?
ᐃᓱᒪᒋᔪᓐᓇᖅᕕᒋᕙᒋᑦ. ᐱᐅᓕᕙᒋᑦ
ᖁᑭᐅᑎᓄᑦ.
ᐱᐅᓯᒋᐊᖅᐸᒋᑦ.
ᐃᑯᒪᒧᑦ ᑭᓯᐊᓂ ᓴᓇᕕᒃᓴᐅᕗᖅ ᓴᕕᖁᔭᑦᑎᐊᕙᖕᒥᒃ.

ᑕᐃᒪᐃᓪᒪᑦ,
ᐃᑭᕈᓗᓚᐅᓇᑦ,

ᐃᑭᕈᓗᓚᐅᓇᑦ.

Manifest

The wooded quiet groans
like a ship upon the storm.
Planks creaking, defecting intact.
Imagine, the nerve of boards
to hit back.

Uppity. Do they know not?
Do they cower not
before their betters?
Seize them.
Bind them to the prow, let them
break waves in a new era
gasping for air.
We shall teach them to tremble.

Camouflaged maple leaves
zip tie and stand by.
Stylish shock troops to Canada goose
step throats.

Does this show of force prove not
how much I love them?
How many volts does it take to show that I care?
That I forgive you. That I redeem you
with bullets.
Refine you.
Only the test of fire makes fine steel.

So,

burn motherfucker,

burn.

ᐃᔨᕋᖅᑐᖅᑕᓂᒃ ᐅᖃᐅᓯᖃᔾᔮᙱᓐᓂᕋᐅᑦ

ᓇᐹᖅᑐᖃᕐᕕᐅᑉ ᐃᑭᐊᖓᓂ ᓯᕐᓗᐊᖅᑕᖃᖅᐳᖅ.
ᓂᓪᓕᐊᔪᖃᖅᐳᖅ ᐅᖃᐅᔭᐃᑦ ᐊᑖᓂ.
ᐃᓪᓗᕋᓛᑦ ᐊᑖᑕᖏᓐᓄᑦ ᑐᓂᔭᐅᕗᑦ
ᐃᔅᓴᒃᑎᖅᓯᒪᔪᑦ ᒑᓯᒧᑦ.

ᐊᓯᐊᓄᑦ ᖀᕕᐊᓇᑦ.
ᐱᖃᑕᐅᓕᖅᑕᐃᓖᑦ.

ᓂᙵᐅᒪᓂᖅᑕᖃᖅᐳᖅ
ᓂᖓᕐᓂᖅᑕᖃᖅᐳᕐᓗ.
        ᖀᐊᔪᑦ ᓱᓪᓗᒃᑰᖅᐳᑦ.
ᖀᐊᔪᑦ ᓄᒫᓱᖕᓂᖏᑦ ᑐᓴᖅᓴᐅᕗᑦ ᐃᓪᓗᕈᓯᕐᒥᑦ ᖃᓂᒋᔭᑦᑎᓐᓂᒃ
ᓂᐱᖃᙱᑦᑎᐊᖅᐳᖅ.

ᓴᒡᓗᕕᒋᒃᑭᑦ ᐊᐅᓚᒃᑭᓪᓗ.
ᑐᓴᐅᒪᑎᒃᑭᑦ ᓯᓚᐃᕐᓇᓗᒥᓪᓗ.
ᐊᑐᕐᓂᕐᓗᒃᑎᑦ ᐃᓄᖕᓂᒃ
ᐃᔨᖅᓯᕙᙱᒻᒪᑖ ᐱᓂᕐᓗᒃᑕᖏᓐᓂᒃ?

ᑐᓴᐅᒪᑎᑦᑎᔩᑦ ᐃᖅᑯᓪᓕᐅᑎᖃᖃᑦᑕᙱᓐᓂᖏᑦ
ᐋᓐᓂᕐᓇᖅᑐᒥᒃ ᐱᕈᐃᔭᓂᒃ ᐊᕐᔭᒥᒃ.
ᐸᐅᓯᒪᔪᑦ ᐱᕈᖅᓲᕕᑦ ᐊᖏᓪᓕᕙᓪᓕᐊᕗᓪᓕ
ᐱᕈᖅᑐᑦ ᐊᑭᕋᖅᑐᕐᓂᕐᒥ.

NDA

There's a basement in the forest.
There's moaning beneath the leaves.
The cabins go to their fathers
soaked in gasoline.

Look the other way.
Don't get involved.

There's anger
and there's violence.
        Sobbing down the hall.
The wailing gloom from an adjacent room
makes no noise at all.

Gaslight and gatekeep.
Disseminate and mislead.
Does not the abuser
silence his misdeeds?

Media blacked out patches
painfully nourish ashes.
Charred seedbeds grow wild instead
raised in adversity.

ᐅᔾᔨᕆᙱᑦᑕᓂᒃ ᐅᖃᐅᔾᔪᐅᓂᖅ

ᖁᔪᑦᑖᓪᓚᐊᑦ ᓇᑲᑎᖅᑕᐅᕗᑦ ᖁᓚᓃᓚᖅᑕᐅᓪᓗᑎᒃ.
ᓇᐹᖅᑑᑉ ᒥᖅᑯᙳᐊᖏᑦ ᑲᑎᖅᓱᖅᓯᒪᒋᕗᒃ ᑐᒃᓯᐊᕈᑎᒃᓴᑦ ᐳᖅᑐᓯᓪᓗᑎᒃ.
ᐳᔫᖅᐳᑦ ᐃᑯᐊᓚᔪᑦ ᐅᓇᑕᕐᓂᐅᕗᑦ ᐊᑕᓂᐅᖃᑎᒌᖕᓄᑦ
ᑐᙵᕙᖃᖅᑐᖅ ᐃᖅᓯᓵᕆᓂᕐᒧᑦ ᐊᖅᔨᙳᖅᑎᑦᑎᓂᕐᒧᓪᓗ
ᐊᖅᓵᖅᓯᓂᐅᕗᖅ ᐱᔪᓐᓇᐅᑎᓂᒃ ᐅᕙᓂᖃᑎᒌᙱᑦᑕᓂᒃ ᐅᒥᐊᙳᓂᕐᒧᑦ.
ᑐᖁᕋᖅᑖᓗᐃᑦ ᓇᖀᓴᖅᑕᐅᕗᓪᓗ,
ᓱᕈᓚᑭᐊᖅᓴᕐᓂᒃᑯᑦ ᖀᒥᖕᓂᒃᑯᓪᓗ,
ᐃᒡᒋᐊᕗᑦ ᒥᓇᐊᖅᓴᕐᓂᐅᓴᓚᖅᐳᑦ ᐱᑦᑎᐊᖅᑕᐅᙱᓐᓂᑦᑎᓐᓄᑦ
ᓇᓗᓇᐃᖅᓯᓂᐊᖅᐹ ᐃᓅᖃᑎᑮᒐᓱᖕᓂᑦᑎᓐᓂᒃ ᐊᒃᓱᕈᕐᓇᖅᑐᓂᒃ?
ᑖᒃᑯᐊ ᐅᕈᑦᑎᓐᓄᑦ ᖃᕙᐊᕈᓐᓇᙱᑦᑐᑦ ᐅᒥᐊᖑᓚᙱᓪᓗᑎᒃ.

ᐃᓅᖃᑎᑮᖕᓂᑦ ᐃᓛᒃᑰᖓᕗᑦ. ᑐᙵᕗᑦ ᑐᑭᓯᐅᒪᓂᕐᓄᑦ ᐊᔾᔨᒌᙱᑦᑐᓄᑦ.
ᐃᖅᑲᖅᑐᐃᓂᖅ ᓱᓚ ᒪᓚᒃᑕᐅᕗᖅ. ᐃᒻᒥᓅᓐᓇᖅ ᐃᓱᒪᓂᐅᕗᖅ ᐃᓛᒃᑰᖓᖕᒪᑦ
ᐱᓂᖅᑰᑕᐅᔪᓐᓇᖅᑐᓂᒃ ᐃᓱᒫᓗᙱᓐᓂᖅ ᖃᓄᐃᓚᒃ ᑐᑭᓯᐅᒪᔭᐅᔪᓐᓇᖅᐳᖅ.
ᐊᖏᖅᑐᖅ ᐱᓂᖅᓗᖕᓂᖅᓂᒃ ᓄᓇᖅᑲᖅᑳᖅᓯᒪᔪᓂᒃ.
ᓂᐱᖏᓐᓂᒃ ᐊᖅᑳᖅᓯᓲᖅ ᑭᖑᓚᑎᓐᓄᑦ ᑎᑭᑦᑐᒋᑦ,
ᐱᑕᖃᙱᓐᓂᐅᓂᖁᐃᕗᖅ ᓲᖑᓴᖕᓂᒃᑯᑦ ᐊᓯᕈᖅᑎᑦᑎᓇᓱᖕᓂᕐᒥᒃ.

ᐊᖓᔪᖅᑳᖏᓐᓂᒃ ᐊᑭᕋᖅᑐᓚᕐᓂᖅ ᓄᖑᓴᖅᑕᐅᕈᓪᓚ ᐱᕈᓗᐊᓚᐅᙱᓐᓂᖕᒐ
ᕿᒻᒥᑦ ᑐᖁᑕᐅᓲᖑᕗᑦ ᓄᓇᓕᖕᓄᑦ ᑕᑯᒃᓴᐅᓪᓗᑎᒃ.
ᐊᑐᕐᓂᕐᓗᖕᓂᐅᕗᖅ ᐱᔪᓐᓇᐅᑎᓂᒃ ᐃᒻᒥᓂᒃ ᐋᓐᓂᕐᓂᖅ ᐃᓗᐊᖅᓯᖁᓪᓗᒍ.
ᓇᐹᖅᑐᑦ ᐅᖃᐅᔾᔪᙳᐊᖏᑦ ᐳᔫᖅᐳᑦ ᒪᓂᒪᑐᐃᓐᓇᕈᒪᙱᓐᓂᕐᒥᒃ
ᐃᑯᐊᓚᔪᒧᑦ ᓄᖑᑕᐅᔪᓐᓇᙱᑦᑐᒥᒃ.

Subliminal

Trees stack like cordwood.
Spruce boughs pile high in sacrifice.
The smoky immolation of a nation-to-nation
built on intimidation and incineration
of rights deemed irrelevant to racist development.
How much Death and disparagement,
contempt and malevolence,
before deep throat contractions to systemic imbalances
define our interactions with our own complex complexions?
Who can't even look us back in the face without resentment.

Relationships are biased. Another frame of reference.
Another's judgment reflected. Subjectively non-objective.
Ignoring consequences has certain connotations.
Condones vicious offences on Indigenous Nations.
Silences victims for generations,
the denied violence of assimilation.

Destroy sedition before it sets.
Put down an animal in public.
Abuse power to ease the pain.
Pine needles smoulder defiant aromas
resistant to the flame.

ᑕᒪᓐᓇ ᐊᑕᓂᐅᖅᑲᑎᒌᑦ ᐊᑭᕋᖕᒋᓐᓄᑦ ᐋᔾᖅᑲᑎᒌᖕᓂᐅᒐᖅ
ᓇᑐᓇᐃᖅᓯᓂᐅᒐᖅ ᓄᓇᖅᑲᖅᓂᖅᒥᒃ, ᒪᓕᒐᖅᓂᒃ ᓱᕋᐃᓂᐅᒐᖅ ᐊᑭᕋᖅᑐᖅᑐᒍ.
ᐳᑭᖅᑕᓖᑦ ᐸᖅᑭᓲᒐᑦ ᑮᓇᐅᔭᓕᐅᕈᑎᓂᒃ:

ᐱᖁᔭᐅᓯᒪᙱᑦᑐᓂᒃ, ᐋᔾᖅᑲᑎᒌᒍᑕᐅᓯᒪᙱᑦᑐᓂᒃ, ᐊᖕᒋᕈᑕᐅᓯᒪᙱᑦᑐᓂᒃ.

ᑖᒃᑯᐊ ᐱᓂᐊᖅᐳᖅ ᐱᔪᒪᔭᑐᐃᓐᓇᖕᒋᓐᓂᒃ.
ᑕᕝᕙᓕ ᓈᒻᒪᒋᔭᑐᐊᓗᕙᐃᑦ
ᓲᖅᑯᖅᑐᖅᕕᒋᒍᑦᑎᒍᑦ.
ᐊᑕᓂᐅᖅᑲᑎᒌᑦ ᐋᔾᖅᑲᑎᒌᖕᓂᖕᒋᑦ ᓴᓪᓗᓂᐅᒐᑦ
ᑕᐃᒪᙵᓕᒫᖅ ᐊᖅᓵᖅᓯᖅᑲᑦᑕᖅᓂᐊᖅᐸᑕ
ᐱᔭᓇᐊᖅᑲᖅᑕᑦᑎᓐᓂᒃ.

This nation-to-nation hostage negotiation
acknowledges land, criminalizes dissent.
Police protect the tenets of industry:

Without permission, consultation, or consent.

They will do as they please.
The only position they respect
is when we are on our knees.
A nation-to-nation will always be deceit
so long as they keep taking
whatever it is we need.

ᓇᐹᖅᑐᖃᕐᕕᖕᒥ ᐊᕙᓗᓕᐊᖑᓯᒪᔪᖅ

ᓇᐹᖅᑐᖃᕐᕕᒃ ᐅᑭᐅᖑᑎᓪᓗᒍ
ᖃᔅᓲᕐᓇᖅᑐᐊᓘᕗᖅ ᑕᑯᒥᓇᖅᑐᓂ.
ᐃᓴᕐᕈᑕᑦ ᐅᖁᒪᐃᓪᓕᓯᒪᔪᑦ ᐊᐳᒻᒧᑦ
ᓂᕕᖓᕗᑦ ᐊᓄᓇᕐᒥ.
ᐳᐃᒍᖅᓴᐅᙱᑦᑐᑦ ᑐᓗᒐᑦ
ᓇᒧᓇᐃᖅᓯᕗᑦ ᐊᓚᒃᑲᕐᓂᕐᓂᒃ,

*H*ᐊᐃ.
*H*ᐊᐃ, ᐃᓂᖁᓇᖏᑦᑐᕈᓘᒃ. *H*ᐊᐃ, ᐃᓂᖁᓇᖏᑦᑐᕐᔭᐊᖅ.
ᐄ, ᐃᕝᕕᑦ.
ᐅᓇ ᓇᐹᖅᑐᖃᕐᕕᑦ ᓇᒧᓇᐃᖅᓯᕗᖅ ᓈᓚᑦᑎᐊᓚᐅᙱᓐᓂᕐᓂᒃ.
ᓈᓚᑦᑎᐊᓚᐅᙱᓐᓂᕐᓂᒃ ᐃᓄᖕᓄᑦ ᓴᓇᓯᒪᙱᑦᑐᓂᒃ.
ᐃᔾᔪᕐᓇᐃᑦᑐᓂᒃ ᐃᔾᔪᕐᓇᐃᙱᑦᑐᓂᒡᓗ.
ᐃᓂᖁᓇᖏᓗᐊᓇᕌᑎᓪᓗ.

ᑐᓗᒐᑦ ᑎᖏᕗᑦ,
ᖄᖃᓚᕗᑦ ᓇᐹᑐᐃᑦ ᐊᑯᓐᓂᖏᒍᑦ.
ᑲᑕᒐᖅᑎᑦᑎᕗᑦ ᐊᐳᒥᒃ ᐃᓴᕐᕈᔭᖕᓂᑦ
ᐊᐳᒥᓪᓗ ᑖᒃᑯᐊ ᓂᐅᖓᕗᑦ
ᑎᐹᕿᑦᑎᐊᖅᑐᑎᒡᓗ ᐊᓄᕆᔮᕐᒥ.

ᐃᓪᓕᓂᑦ ᐊᑐᕆᒃᓴᐅᖏᑦᑐᑦ ᐊᐅᔭᒃᑯᑦ
ᐊᑐᕆᓂᓕᐅᖑᕗᑦ ᐅᑭᐅᒃᑯᑦ.
ᖁᔭᓈᖅᑕᐅᓯᒪᔪᑦ, ᓲᕐᓗ,
ᐃᓱᖃᖏᑦᑐᒧᑦ ᐅᓪᓗᒧᓪᓗ.
ᕿᔪᑦ ᐃᓗᕕᕐᓄᑦ ᓇᒧᓇᐃᒃᑯᑕᑦ ᐃᓵᒃᓯᒪᕗᑦ
ᓯᕿᓂᕐᒧᑦ ᓂᐱᓕᖅᑐᒧᑦ.

Forest Henge

A wall of winter forest
draws you in like a magic eye.
Snow-burdened branches
dip in the wind.
Indelible ravens
announce your arrival,

Hey.
Hey, Ugly.   Hey, Big Ugly.
Yeah, you.
This forest finds you in contempt.
In contempt of all that is natural.
Of the Sacred and Profane.
          Of not being too handsome.

They take wing,
cackling through jack pine.
Releasing snowy boughs
that mottle the landscape
and perfume the breeze.

Trails impassable in summer
are at your leisure come winter.
Abandoned, as it were, for
forever and a day.
Birch headstones reaching
before the setting sun.

ᐃᒡᓗᕋᓛᑦ ᓂᓚᒃᓯᒪᕗᑦ
ᐃᒪᕈᔅᓴᐅᓚᐅᖅᑐᑦ ᓲᖅᑯᕐᒧᑦ ᑎᑭᐅᒪᔪᒧᑦ ᐃᖅᑲᐅᒪᓂᕐᒧᑦ
ᐅᑕᖅᑭᔪᒧᑦ
ᓯᑯᐃᕐᓂᐊᕐᓂᖓᓂᒃ ᑰᒃ ᐊᖏᕐᕋᒧᑦ ᐅᓯᔭᐅᓛᕐᒪᑕ ᐅᒥᐊᕐᒧᑦ.
ᐃᓗᕕᖅᓯᓂᖅ ᐃᒪᕕᖕᒥ!
ᓇᐹᖅᑑᑉ ᒥᖅᑯᙳᐊᖏᓐᓄᑦ ᐱᐅᓕᔭᐅᕗᒍᑦ

ᐃᖏᕐᕋᑎᓪᓗᑕ ᑰᒃᑐᒧᑦ.

Cabins murked in ice
flood knee deep in memory
waiting
for the breakup to ferry them home.
A burial at sea!
As spruce boughs preserve us

as we drift downstream.

Artwork by Erica Jacque

ᓴᐃᒥᓯ ᕗᐊᓐᓂᐊᐃ

ᐃᓄᒃ ᐱᕈᖅᓯᒪᔪᖅ ᑎᐊᓇᓐᑕᐃ ᓄᓇᖓᓐᓂ, ᓴᐃᒥᓯ ᕗᐊᓐᓂᐊᐃ ᑎᑎᕋᖅᑲᑦᑕᖅᓯᒪᕗᖅ *Inuit Art Quarterly*-ᒥ, *Red Rising*-ᒥ, *Northern Public Affairs*-ᒥ, ᐊᒻᒪᓗ ᐅᖅᑲᓕᒫᓗᕐᒥ *Coming Home: Stories from the Northwest Territories*. ᓄᑲᖓ, ᓯᐱᑎ ᑐᓗᒐᖅ ᐃᕙᓗᐊᕐᔪᒃ ᕗᐊᓐᓂᐊᐃ, ᑎᑎᖅᑐᒐᖅᓯᒪᕗᖅ ᓴᐃᒥᓯᐅᑉ ᑎᑎᕋᖅᑕᖏᓐᓂᒃ *Inuit Art Quarterly*-ᒥ ᒪᕿᐊᖅᑎᖅᑐᓂ. ᓴᐃᒥᓯ ᐃᓇᑕᐅᓚᐅᖅᐳᖅ ᑎᑎᕋᖁᓴᐅᑦᓗᓂ 2018-ᒥ ᐊᒻᒪᓗ 2020-ᒥ Northwords Writers Festival-ᒥ ᐊᒻᒪᓗ ᑭᖑᓪᓕᐅᓚᐅᖅᑐᖅ 2018-ᒥ Sally Manning Award-ᒥᒃ ᓄᓇᖃᖅᑳᖅᓯᒪᔪᑦ ᐅᓂᒃᑳᓕᐅᕐᓂᕐᒧᑦ ᓱᓕᔪᓂᒃ. ᓄᓇᖃᖅᐳᖅ ᑎᑉᕚᑦᓴ/Fort Smith ᐊᑯᓐᓂᖓᓂ Salt River ᓄᓇᖃᖅᑳᖅᓯᒪᔪᑦ ᐊᒻᒪᓗ Smith's Landing ᓄᓇᖃᖅᑳᖅᓯᒪᔪᑦ, ᐊᒻᒪᓗ South Slave Metis Nation.

Jamesie Fournier

An Inuk raised in Denendeh, Jamesie Fournier's work has appeared in *Inuit Art Quarterly*, *Red Rising* magazine, *Northern Public Affairs*, and the anthology *Coming Home: Stories from the Northwest Territories*. His brother, Zebede Tulugaq Evaluardjuk-Fournier, illustrated his last two projects with *Inuit Art Quarterly*. Jamesie was guest author at the 2018 and 2020 NorthWords Writers Festivals and a runner-up for the 2018 Sally Manning Award for Indigenous Creative Non-Fiction. He lives in Thebacha/Fort Smith between Salt River First Nation, Smith's Landing First Nation, and the South Slave Métis Nation.

INHABIT
MEDIA
IQALUIT • TORONTO